How to get a tax refund and pay less tax in future

An employee's guide to tax allowances hidden in plain view

By Wisdom Da Costa B.SC, FCCA, AMCT

First paperback edition printed 2013 in the United Kingdom

Published by A Star Accounting Services Ltd

A catalogue record for this book is available from the British Library.

ISBN 978-0-9926716-1-7

Although every precaution has been taken in the preparation of this book, the publisher and author assume no responsibility for errors or omissions. Neither is any liability assumed for damages resulting from the use of this information contained herein.

For more copies of this book email info@astaraccounting.co.uk Tel: +44 1753 840040 Website: www.astaraccounting.co.uk

Acknowledgements

Thank you to all who helped to publish this book including God, Chris Pereira, Carole Da Costa, Judith Forster & Jonathan Da Costa, and a special word of thanks to Lord Palmer of Childs Hill FCA, OBE. Without each of you, this project wouldn't have happened.

Dedication

This book is dedicated to the 30 million employees and directors in the UK.

"An inheritance gained hurriedly at the beginning will not be blessed in the end"

Proverbs Chapter 20, Verse 21

Comments about this book

"Wisdom Da Costa has produced a book which I am sure will enable many people to better organise their tax affairs and to take advantage of allowances, expenses and deductions which can be used to reduce tax liabilities."

Lord Palmer of Childs Hill, OBE FCA

The book contains useful information and advice and sample template letters that readers will find useful. I commend the book to you."

John Richards OBE, International Banker

Contents

What's in this book?

Find out who the author is, who he has worked for, how he has legitimately helped clients save millions of pounds in tax, and why he wrote this self-help book to help employees like you pay less tax.

We all want to pay the right amount of tax, but have you ever wondered if you are paying too much? In the Introduction, you will discover if you might have overpaid tax and if so, how much that could be worth, and how to get it refunded.

Throughout this book, I try to make tax simpler and more understandable, which will help you learn more about the scope of this book, how to get the most from it, and where to find the real gems hidden away in the confusing minefield of all-things-tax. I will also introduce the **Quickclaim** service which will simplify the process to a few simple clicks and I will tell you where to go to access this service.

I want to make sure that you are as fully empowered as possible. This chapter sets out some of the key principles to follow to help you, as an employee, make successful claims to HMRC for tax you have overpaid. It will also help you apply the Key Principles to your personal situation by leading you through some practical exercises.

Chapter Two Specific Allowances - Costs and Expenses You Can Claim   **p 15**

Discover Seventeen allowances that you might be able to claim for. Yes, 17! I will explain in more detail what you can claim and under what conditions, when it would apply to you and how to put a value to your claim, reveal some top tax tips, and point you to more resources and tools to help you.

Chapter Three Capital Allowances, Loan Interest and Other Tax Effective Payments   **p 33**

The list doesn't end there, and in this chapter I will show you more allowances you can claim, including some of the most powerful tools available to employees. I have aimed to simplify tax as far as possible, but as some of these items are still complex, I have taken time to explain how to make a successful and valid claim. This section also contains examples to help you work through your learning, and points you towards more online resources available to you.

Chapter Four Industry and Job-specific Allowances – Costs and Expenses You Can Claim   **p 52**

Did you know that there are guaranteed allowances available for certain professions and industries? Find out if your job or industry is included, and if so, what you could make a guaranteed claim for. If you can claim for these items then you will receive a tax refund worth £hundreds or even £thousands now, and you will also pay less tax in future.

HMRC and the government do not make life easy for employees, and there are a number of hidden snares and pitfalls along the way. However, there are also opportunities to watch out for and here I set out some of the tacit rules of the road. You may be surprised by what you read!

Here I show you how to make your claim. There are detailed examples provided, including templates to make sure you don't forget anything. You will be directed to online resources available to you, many without charge. I also inform you about the deadlines for making successful claims.

Can't be bothered to write your own Claim Letter? Then copy one of ten examples, templates, or blanks here. With instructions to simplify your life.

Are you looking for something specific? Use these lists to navigate quickly through the book.

Find allowances and tax tips specific to your job, or similar roles, quickly by using this comprehensive Index; Search for higher allowances for say related types of jobs; Dig for gold.

About the Author

Wisdom Da Costa is a Qualified Accountant, Corporate Treasurer, and Schoolteacher. He began his accounting career with Touche Ross then eventually took a number of senior finance roles within SITA UK. He currently owns an accountancy practice in the South East of England.

As an Accountant, Wisdom has thirty years experience helping individuals and businesses pay less tax, cutting tens of millions of pounds off their tax bills by developing and implementing innovative tools to improve their case, and by presenting information effectively. As a Corporate Treasurer, he has developed sound and effective ways to assess and protect against financial risk whilst also dealing with the more mundane aspects of the job. As a Teacher, he has developed and trained teenagers, helping to release their potential.

Wisdom's skill is to uncover the possibilities and then empower people to benefit.

People just like you.

The UK tax system is unnecessarily complex, requiring accountants to make sense of it all, and find paths through minefields full of potential hazards. Companies can afford an accountant, but most employees can't. Wisdom has packaged his knowledge and expertise into an easy-to-access book and website to help you navigate through the system and help save you money.

Wisdom lives with his wife, two dogs and children in Windsor. In his spare time he enjoys windsurfing, watching Reading FC, working in the community and spending time with friends and family.

Introduction

Are you paying the right amount of tax? Would you like to pay less tax?

In the UK, 30 million employees are unaware that they are entitled to claim allowances set by the Government and HMRC, which, over the long term, will significantly reduce their tax bills. Not only that, but the majority of them are also entitled to refunds in cash of between £70 and £2,500 due to previously unclaimed allowances over the last five years! Thousands of others could also make valid additional claims for even more than £2,500.

From the top position of director of a company, to the employee in any capacity, there are up to twenty-one different types of costs, expenses and allowances you can claim to offset against your yearly tax bill. So if you haven't made a claim before and you are entitled to one, this book could be worth a lot of money to you both now and in the future.

A sizeable tax refund, and a life or less tax, could be only a few pages and a few clicks away!

Making it easy

Tax can be complex. It is frequently full of jargon and unintelligible phrases making it difficult terrain to navigate through to the final destination. Tax rules that apply to the 30 million employees and directors living in the UK can also be overly restrictive and longwinded, compared to reliefs available to people liable for other types of tax.

So to save you the trouble, I have sifted through page after page of rules, regulations and laws, and then processed the information to produce for you a user-friendly and concise guide to what you are entitled to claim.

This is very much a 'can do' book, and my aim is to be your guide you every step of the way. I recommend that you work through the book methodically, making a note of the tax tips that are relevant to you as you read through, until you arrive at the point when you are ready to make a claim.

Watch out for extra items marked **"Tax Tip"**, or **"Tax Gem"**. Tax Tips will help you avoid a pitfall, or point out what to do to make your claim more certain; Tax Gems are very powerful tips that allow you to maximise your tax refund, and minimise any tax payable.

The 'How to Make a Claim' section marks the end of your journey with a step-by-step guide to help you use the information specific to your requirements that you have noted to make a claim. This section includes forms and templates of the letter you will need to send to the HMRC. It's as easy as that! The book also tells you which boxes to fill in if HMRC insist that you have to submit a Self Assessment tax return (**SAR**), using HMRC's SAR forms SA102 for 2013 (Employment pages), and SA100 (Tax return 2013) as references; watch out for text [*in square brackets, underlined and in italics*]; you can find a copy of forms SA102, and SA100 for 2013 at http://taxrefundbook1.accountingwisdom.com.

How the website can help

By registering on the website you will be able to access, free of charge, a range of articles and useful resources to help you, including forms and spread sheets, and receive email updates on issues that may affect you. But don't worry we will try and keep the emails to a minimum.

Watch out for the **Quickclaim** mark later in the book next to appropriate sections. If you see this mark, and have only these types of expenses, you can use the web application at http://taxrefundbook1.accountingwisdom.com to make a quick automated claim, so speeding up the process. For a small fee, this service will write your claim letter for you using information you are prompted to provide. Then all you have to do is print, sign, and post it to the address that will be provided to you. For more information, go to http://taxrefundbook1.accountingwisdom.com.

This book and the website are not intended to be comprehensive or detailed manuals on the intricacies of tax regulations, laws, or practices. Instead they offer a simplified overview of what employees and directors are entitled to claim, and how to go about claiming it. If your tax needs are particularly complex, or you need further help or information which is not available in the book or on the website, I recommend that you seek help from a qualified accountant.

Be aware that tax laws and HMRC's practices change regularly. We will cover key changes in future editions & updates of this book, but for now, remember to check with HMRC, and sign up to our email update service at http://taxrefundbook1.accountingwisdom.com.

This is the first in a series of publications designed to help streamline and reduce your tax bills. Future publications will advise on other key issues such as what to do if you own a property and rent it, how to go about starting up a business, what are the areas to look out for if you are self-employed or you run or own a small or medium sized business, and how to invest your cash wisely including tax-effective savings schemes and purchasing shares in companies and family businesses.

You can sign up to our news feed to hear about new books and ideas to help you get your tax right at http://taxrefundbook1.accountingwisdom.com.

Finally, remember you are responsible for any false, incorrect or misleading claims you make in the information that you supply to HMRC, so let's keep it real!

Chapter One

Key Principles and How to Apply Them

Take a moment to think about your occupation. What do you do? What is your title and job description? Where do you do it and what tools do you use? Are you in a role that requires you pay job related costs personally, even if your employer reimburses you at a later date?

Learning to think about these things is important as you begin to work out what expenses you can claim. Keeping records of this information, together with any evidence or paperwork to back it up is extremely useful should the HMRC come back to you with any questions regarding your claim. Producing authentic proof of costs and expenses gives you a watertight position if doubt is cast over the claims you submit.

So what are the Key Principles?

Her Majesty's Revenue and Customs (HMRC) states that:

"A deduction from earnings is allowed for an amount if (a) the employee is obliged to incur and pay it as holder of the employment, and (b) the amount is incurred wholly, exclusively and necessarily in the performance of the duties of the employment."

They call this 'The General Rule' and it is used to clarify when and why an employee is entitled to tax relief from HMRC. In simpler terms it means that you can get tax relief for costs that you have been obliged to pay in connection with your role. You need to have proof that you have paid for each item and, with the exception of 'travel and subsistence', the expenditure should not have any material personal benefit to you. The good news is, if you can get tax relief on a cost, you will pay less tax, or if you have already paid it e.g. through PAYE, then you can get a refund of the tax you have paid that relates to the tax relief.

So when are you obliged by your employer to incur a cost?

Usually this will be if there is a clause in either your contract of employment, or some other related document such as your employer's Employee Manual. This may also occur if it is 'common practice' to make such payments and was necessary to enable you to perform the key duties required by your role.

The costs that you pay, and from which you can claim tax relief, will depend on your particular job and working practices: how your job is done. However, there are some costs that can relate to all forms of employment and those will be made clear later on in the book in Chapters 2 and 3.

Record keeping

You are required to keep good records, as HMRC may ask you to prove your claim. They should include receipts, explanations, and details of your contract of employment and job description at the time. Practically, you should keep records for up to 5 years.

You can use technology to help you keep clear records of your costs, expenses, and allowance claims, and this can include photographic evidence as well as original copies. To get you started, apps, electronic spread sheets, work sheets, and reviews are available online at http://taxrefundbook1.accountingwisdom.com.

How much can I claim?

You can claim expenses, costs, and allowances up to the value of your income from that employer for the year. In other words, you cannot claim **more** than the money you earned over the last year.

Also, you have to reduce your claim by any amount that your employer repaid to you. So, if your employer repaid you nothing, or reimbursed you a sum less than the money you paid, or the specific allowance you are taking advantage of, then you can make a claim to HMRC.

See **Tricks and Tips** (Chapter Five) for further help using Capital Allowances to create an employment income loss.

What about P11Ds?

You can get tax relief for business expenses that you have paid, a) where your employer reimbursed you, and which have been included on your P11D, or b) if you employer either did not reimburse you at all, or only reimbursed you in part.

For more information about P11Ds, go to Chapter Five.

Keep these Key Principles in mind, and remember to refer back to them as you read through the rest of this book.

Practical exercise

- Obtain a copy of the following documents: your job description; your contract of employment; any other documents that may define what you have to do, and/or how you do your job.
- Consider your actual job title. Is it correct? If not, write down what you actually do and redefine it accordingly.
- Using your actual job description as a starting point, list down all the tasks you perform in your job.
- Which of these tasks are key to your role?
- Go through your job description and contract of employment, to see if there are any costs which you are actually **required**, or effectively

obliged (e.g. because your employer does not pay them) to pay to enable you to do your job.

- Make a list of all the types of costs you **actually** pay in relation to your job.
- Which costs relate to the primary tasks of your actual role?
- Keep a copy of all your workings, and the documents above, in case HMRC need to see them, as this will be your documented evidence to claim your entitlement to tax relief.

Wash, rinse, repeat

If you repeat this exercise once you have worked through Chapters 2 & 3 you will be able to get a more accurate list of the expenses you can claim, and tie it more closely to your documented evidence of your entitlement to tax relief.

What's coming next?

So, you can actually claim ANY appropriate work related expenses to reduce the tax you pay.

To help you get your head around what might be "appropriate", in the next three chapters we will reveal 22 categories of expenses and allowances that you might be able to claim to reduce your annual tax liability, and earn you some welcome "cash back" from HMRC.

Chapter Two

Specific Allowances, Costs and Expenses You Can Claim

This chapter will give you a list of what you may be able to claim for and what conditions make a successful claim more likely. We will look at how to put a value to your application where the value is not the amount of money you spent on the item. If HMRC require you to complete a Self Assessment Tax Return (SAR), at the end of each Section, [*in square brackets, underlined and in italics*], you will see which box, on which page of your SAR you need to fill in.

You can potentially claim allowances, costs and expenses in the following areas if you have followed the key principles outlined in the previous chapter in addition to any other more detailed rules specifically related to an item below.

Key categories pertaining to specific claims

Chapter Two

1. Assistants wages

2. Blind employee's guide dog

3. Books

4. Car washing

5. Clothing (Use the **Quickclaim** service)

6. Club subscriptions

7. Education and training

8. Entertainment

9. Losses and commercial costs

10. Professional fees and subscriptions (Use the **Quickclaim** service)

11. Telephone costs

12. Tools and equipment (Use the **Quickclaim** service)

13. Travelling: allowance for using your own vehicle (MAR)

14. Travelling: public transport, planes, etc

15. Travelling: accommodation & subsistence

16. Use of home and working from home

17. Other costs

Chapter Three

Capital allowances and loan interest

18. Capital allowances on plant and machinery used

19. Interest on certain loans

Other important tax effective payments (do not miss this!)

20. Gift aid donations

21. Personal Pension payments

Over the next two chapters we will look at each of these categories in more detail before we reveal the 22 item, in "**Chapter Four, Industry and Job-specific Allowances – Costs and Expenses You Can Claim.**"

1. Assistants wages

Payments of wages to an assistant are allowed if you are 'paid solely by results' or where your duties of employment stated in your contract require you to 'engage and remunerate assistants to do some of the work'. This could cover anything from a sub-postmaster to a clergyman. Wages must be paid and be reasonable for the work done.

Be aware however that you must not be seen as an employer for PAYE purposes. This would require you to register with HMRC for PAYE, operate a payroll, deduct PAYE, and submit onerous and copious quantities of information to HMRC. Also, as an employer, you would be required to pay the additional Employer's National Insurance contributions. This is currently around an additional 14% of the wage you paid your assistant.

Tax Tip 1 – you will be required to register as an employer and operate a PAYE payroll, if you are a) paying the assistant at or above the PAYE threshold, b) your employee already has another job, c) they are receiving a state, company or private pension, d) you are paying them at or above the National Insurance Lower Earnings Limit, or e) if you're providing them with employee benefits. You can claim the actual amount you paid for wages and payroll taxes. For further information please refer to http://taxrefundbook1.accountingwisdom.com.

[SAR 'Employment' pages E1 →Employment expenses →Box 20 'Other expenses and capital allowances' or in any similar box.]

2. Blind employee's guide dog

If you are blind (HMRC's expression) and you use a guide dog to aid mobility in your role at work you can claim for the whole cost of keeping and eventually replacing the dog. "The deduction should reflect the reasonable cost of keeping and replacing the guide dog. You should not try to apportion the cost between business and private use." As ever, HMRC may apply a reasonableness test to your claim before they agree it. You can claim the actual amount of costs you paid. For further information please refer to http://taxrefundbook1.accountingwisdom.com.

[SAR 'Employment' pages E1 →Employment expenses →Box 20 'Other expenses and capital allowances' or in any similar box.]

3. Books

You can claim the cost of books you have actually purchased in order to do your job, but only if the expense is wholly, exclusively, and necessarily incurred for the actual performance of your duties. In addition, it has to be an expense that your job (rather than you) requires. For example if you are a teacher who has to buy books for use by pupils in the classroom. You can claim the actual amount you paid.

Training costs are not allowed. See Section 7 late in this chapter on "Education and training"

[SAR 'Employment' pages E1 →Employment expenses →Box 20 'Other expenses and capital allowances' or in any similar box.]

4. Car washing

You can claim for this if your duties require you to keep your car clean. Check your employment contract carefully to see if this is a requirement of your employer. This is particularly likely to be allowable if you are employed as a chauffeur or car valet. You can claim the actual amount you paid.

[SAR 'Employment' pages E1 →Employment expenses →Box 20 'Other expenses and capital allowances' or in any similar box.]

5. Clothing (You can use the **Quickclaim** service for this expense)

If you are required by your employer, or the nature of your job, to wear any form of uniform, specialist clothing or protective clothing then you can normally access two claims:

1. You can claim any costs you paid to purchase the clothing, or to replace that clothing

2. You can claim costs of cleaning and upkeep of that clothing

Uniforms are classed a recognisable full uniform or part of a uniform. Part uniform could be anything from a tabard or tunic worn over your own clothes to an outfit in a specific colour. Clothing can also include items such as overalls, gloves, boots, & helmets depending on your job.

If your employer provides you with dry cleaning, other cleaning facilities or tokens, you must use these first, only then claiming the extra costs over and above your allowance.

You can either claim the actual costs you pay, or for certain professions, you can claim a set allowance each year that you are in that role. You can check if your profession, role, or industry has a fixed allowance by going to Chapter Four, using the Index, or by using the Quickclaim service on the website at http://taxrefundbook1.accountingwisdom.com. The good news is that you can still claim a standard amount of £60 for the laundry costs of cleaning uniforms or protective clothing even if your industry is not listed on the table.

Tax Tip 2 - To help your claim, you should explain to HMRC how you qualify to make this claim, for example why you have to use the clothing you have purchased for work, or why your cleaning and maintenance costs are for example greater than normal. You can use words like protective, safety, but for more information, and worked examples of real life cases, read the articles on the dedicated website at http://taxrefundbook1.accountingwisdom.com.

As always, if you do claim the actual costs you paid, you should keep a copy of the invoices, or receipts in case the HMRC officer asks you for evidence.

[If actual costs: SAR 'Employment' pages E1 → Employment expenses → Box 20 'Other expenses and capital allowances' or in any similar box.]

or

[If a FRE: SAR 'Employment' pages E1 → Employment expenses → Box 18 'Fixed deductions for expenses' or in any similar box.]

6. Club subscriptions

You are allowed to claim costs which include a personal benefit if your personal benefit is only incidental, and if there is a clear business purpose. In other words, if you happen to live in Belfast and need to regularly travel to London for business, it may be that a specific club subscription works out cheaper than staying in hotels.

[SAR 'Employment' pages E1 → Employment expenses → Box 20 'Other expenses and capital allowances' or in any similar box.]

7. Education and training

Tax relief on the costs of education and training including the cost of a particular course, relevant textbooks and materials, and travel and subsistence will be allowed only if

- Training is an intrinsic part of your contractual duties of employment, and

- There is a mandatory requirement for you as the employee to undertake external training as an intrinsic part of the duties of the employment, and
- Failure to complete the training and obtain the qualification will mean that you as the employee will not be able to continue in employment with the employer in the role that would otherwise have been available to you after the qualification.

In other words if your contract of employment says you must, and if failure to do so will mean that you lose your job. You can claim the actual amount you paid.

Unfortunately, tax relief on costs incurred for Continuing Professional Education/Development (CPE or CPD) are not allowed under any circumstances.

*[SAR "Employment" pages E1 →Employment expenses →**Box 20 "Other expenses and capital allowances" or in any similar box.**]*

8. Entertainment

This will be allowed only if the expense

- Has been paid or reimbursed by your employer, and
- If the reimbursed element has been included on your P11D, and
- If your employer is not claiming a tax deduction on the expense.

You can claim the actual amount you paid.

On the whole, it is better not to pay for entertainment on behalf of your company.

Tax Tip 3 – Your Entertainment costs may qualify as subsistence, and thus be "OK". Check Section 15 later in this chapter.

*[SAR "Employment" pages E1 →Employment expenses →**Box 20 "Other expenses and capital allowances" or in any similar box.**]*

9. Losses and commercial costs

You can claim any losses of your employer that you are contractually obliged to suffer (see the Section entitled **"Practical exercise"** in Chapter 1). In other words, you are entitled to claim losses if for example, you are a commercial traveller responsible for bad debts arising from orders you have obtained, or if you are a sub-postmaster and are contractually required to pay back to the Post Office any net cash deficiency (i.e. the balance of deficiencies over excesses).

Tax Tip 4 - Check your contract of employment and your employer's Employee Manual, and make a note of the clauses which oblige you to incur such losses or commercial costs.

*[SAR "Employment" pages E1 →Employment expenses →**Box 20 "Other expenses and capital allowances" or in any similar box.**]*

10. Professional fees and subscriptions (You can use the **Quickclaim**

service for this expense)

You can claim the cost of professional membership fees and subscriptions paid to approved bodies if your duties of employment involve the practice of that profession and if failure to pay the fee will prevent you from practising that profession. Membership of professional bodies, and subscriptions to trades unions are included in this.

HMRC perhaps apply this more generously than the official wording indicates so for more information refer to http://taxrefundbook1.accountingwisdom.com if you wish to check whether the item for which you wish to claim is specifically approved by HMRC. If your union, or professional body is not on the list but a similar organisation is on the list, make a claim, and be willing to argue your case.

You can claim the actual amount you paid.

[SAR "Employment" pages E1 →Employment expenses →Box 19 "Professional fees and subscriptions" or in any similar box.]

11.   Telephone costs

You can claim the cost of business calls made from a landline or mobile phone only where you can identify cost from your itemised bill, or you can claim all of the costs if the phone is used for business purposes alone.

Claims for rental of a telephone line or mobile are allowed if there is a genuine business need and that line is used exclusively for business calls, as, for example, in the case of ministers of religion, teleworkers and 'live-in' care workers.

For home broadband costs, refer to the section below on working from home.

*[SAR "Employment" pages E1 →Employment expenses →**Box 20 "Other expenses and capital allowances" or in any similar box.**]*

12.   Tools & equipment (You can use the **Quickclaim** service for this expense)

If you use tools for your job that your employer does not provide, you can either claim the actual amount you spend each year, **or** you can claim the full amount of any annual Flat Rate Expense (FRE) available to you, even if you only spend £1 on an item.

If your tools cost more than £1000, you should make a claim under Capital Allowances rather than as "expenses of employment." Capital Allowance claims can be very powerful tools. We tell you how to claim Capital Allowances in Chapter Three, and about the power of using them in Chapter Five Tricks and Tips.

To help your claim, you should explain to HMRC how you qualify to make this claim, for example why you have to use the tools you have purchased to do your job, or why your cleaning and maintenance costs are for example greater than normal. For more information, and worked examples of real life cases of people who use their own tools including medical staff, mechanics, pilots & drivers, catering staff, outdoor workers, read the articles on the dedicated website at http://taxrefundbook1.accountingwisdom.com.

You can check if your profession, role or industry has a fixed allowance FRE in one of three ways; 1) By going to Chapter Four entitled '**Industry and job specific allowances costs and expenses you can claim**', or 2) By using the book's helpful Index to search for your job, or by 3) Using the **Quickclaim** service on the website at http://taxrefundbook1.accountingwisdom.com.

Tax Tip 5 – if the amount you spent is more than £1, but less than the FRE, claim the FRE.

Tax Tip 6 – if the amount that you spent is more than the FRE, then claim the actual amount you spent, but remember to keep a list of each item you paid for, and a copy of the receipts See Section entitled "**Record keeping** " in Chapter One.

*[**If actual costs:** SAR "Employment" pages E1 →Employment expenses →Box 20 "Other expenses and capital allowances" or in any similar box.*]

OR

*[**If a FRE:** SAR "Employment" pages E1 →Employment expenses →Box 18 "Fixed deductions for expenses" or in any similar box.]*

13.   Travelling: allowance for using your own vehicle – Mileage Allowance Relief (MAR)

You can claim a Mileage Allowance Relief (MAR) if you use your own car, van, motorcycle, or bicycle to travel for work (excluding commuting between home and work if you are not "called out"). You should claim this allowance instead of the actual cost of fuel, which may probably be lower; MAR is usually higher than the actual cost of fuel, especially for longer journeys, as it also includes an element of insurance, maintenance, and depreciation.

- If you use a car or van, you can currently claim 45p per mile, for the first 10,000 business miles, then 25p per mile for mileage in excess of 10,000.
- If you use a motorcycle, you can currently claim 24p per mile for all miles travelled.
- If you use a bicycle, you can currently claim 20p per mile for all miles travelled.

You should keep a record of each journey you made including the date, departure point, reason for journey, destination, passengers, and miles travelled.

You can find record keeping tools, and check the current MAR rates as they do change periodically, on your dedicated website at http://taxrefundbook1.accountingwisdom.com. The rates quoted above are applicable in 2013/14.

Tax Tip 7 – If your employer does not already pay you an allowance for mileage you can claim the full amount calculated at the rate listed.

Tax Tip 8 – If your employer pays you less than this figure, you can claim the difference between both what HMRC will allow you to claim e.g. at 45p/25p per mile for a car or van, and the actual sum your employer pays you. However if your employer puts the value they pay you on your P11D, claim the full amount of the MAR as an expense.

Tax Gem 1 – You can claim the 10,000 mile rate for <u>each</u> employer you work for in a year i.e. you get a first 10,000 miles higher rate for each employer e.g. if you work for two different employers during the tax year, you can get up to 20,000 miles at the higher 45p rate.

Tax Tip 9 - Check your P11D to see whether your employer has included a value for fuel or MAR, then go to the P11D heading in the Tricks & Tips chapter.

[SAR "Employment" pages E1 →*Employment expenses* →***Box 17 "Business travel and subsistence expenses" or in any similar box.*]

14.   Travelling: public transport, aeroplanes, etc

Where you travel on business in the performance of your duties you can claim travelling costs excluding commuting between home and work. See also Section 15 below. You can claim the actual amount you paid.

You can find more information, tools, and advice on Apps to help you keep a track of expenses at http://taxrefundbook1.accountingwisdom.com.

[SAR "Employment" pages E1 →*Employment expenses* →***Box 17 "Business travel and subsistence expenses" or in any similar box.*]

15.   Travelling: accommodation & subsistence

When you claim travelling costs you can also include what you paid during the journey for hotel accommodation, entertaining, subsistence, meals, tolls, congestion charges, parking fees, business phone calls, fax or photocopying costs. You can claim the actual amount you paid.

Tax Tip 10 – Claim the cost of meals, and light refreshments for yourself e.g. coffee/tea/water, but to be on the safe side and to avoid the pain of a challenge by HMRC, do not claim for alcohol with meals unless the alcohol is provided by the restaurant as part of a set menu.

You can find more information, tools, and advice on Apps to help you keep a track of expenses at http://taxrefundbook1.accountingwisdom.com.

[SAR "Employment" pages E1 →*Employment expenses* →***Box 17 "Business travel and subsistence expenses" or in any similar box.*]**

16.   Use of home and working from home

This is one of the more complex areas to understand, as there are so many variables so you may find it helpful to refer to our worksheet to help you compile your claim, or to use some of the tools and resources available on our website at http://taxrefundbook1.accountingwisdom.com.

What can be claimed?

Generally you can claim the additional element of certain costs that you have to pay, because you are using the home as a place of work.

You can claim for extra gas, electricity, heating costs, and water consumed.

You can also claim for Broadband under certain circumstances (see below for more information), and certain telephone costs (see Section 11 above)

Employees who work from home may not claim Council Tax or rates, rent, water rates, mortgage interest payments, endowment premiums or insurance.

How much can I claim?

There are two options for how much you can claim: you can either claim £4 per week (£18 per month) **or** you can claim the actual extra additional costs or a proportion of the costs after you have worked out the total amounts spent on allowable items.

What about broadband costs?

Broadband costs can only be claimed if you installed the broadband access **after** you started working from home.

Tax Gem 2 – The good news is that you can always claim 100% of your broadband costs from that point on if you pass this test and can prove you did not have broadband before you started working from home!

Some hurdles to overcome

The rules for employees are different, and much stricter, than those for the self-employed. Employees who work from home have to jump over a number hurdles before HMRC will allow them to claim home working costs. However, with some careful planning, which may involve the employer taking action, many people successfully claim the costs of working from their home.

So what are the obstacles?

Hurdle one - If you have a choice whether to work from home or not, then your claim will not be allowed. Conversely, if you do not have a choice and you are required to work from home, your claim will be allowed.

Tax Tip 11 – If you normally work from home, make sure that your employer sets out a **requirement that you work from home** in writing e.g. in your contract of employment.

Tax Tip 12 – If you are required to work from home less frequently, ask your employer to set out in writing a requirement that you work from home when instructed, and also ensure that you get an instruction in writing to work from home when you do work from home.

Hurdle two - You must perform some of your central duties from home.

Tax Tip 13 – Refer to your job description to check what your central duties are given your role and title, and ask your employer to reflect in your central duties, if appropriate, tasks that you perform at home.

Hurdle three - Your duties can't be performed without appropriate facilities.

Hurdle four - Those facilities are not available in your employer's place of work. You will need to be able to prove this.

Tax Tip 14 – For practical purposes this could include if you work too far away from the your 'office', or if your 'office' closes at nights, over weekends etc.

NB Some roles in certain professions are specifically allowed to claim costs for the use of home, for example domiciliary midwives.

You will find spread sheets, work sheets, examples and other resources on our website at http://taxrefundbook1.accountingwisdom.com.

[If actual costs: SAR "Employment" pages E1 →Employment expenses →Box 20 "Other expenses and capital allowances" or in any similar box.]   **OR**

[In a FRE: SAR "Employment" pages E1 →Employment expenses →Box 18 "Fixed deductions for expenses" or in any similar box.]

17.   Other costs

What if you have spent money on items not mentioned here or anywhere else in the following lists that you believe pass the tests under 'Key Principles' and perhaps also the concepts under 'Club subscriptions' (see Section 6 above)?

Well it is possible you may have a valid claim, but you are likely to have to argue your case with HMRC. In other words make a claim, but be prepared to enter into correspondence with them, and also show them why your expenditure is 'wholly, exclusively, and necessarily' required by your role, using your job description and contract of employment as proof.

[SAR "Employment" pages E1 →Employment expenses →Box 20 "Other expenses and capital allowances" or in any similar box.]

Chapter Three

Capital Allowances, Loan Interest and Other Tax Effective Payments

What are Capital Allowances?

Sometimes there is a requirement to spend money on more expensive items such as computers, filing cabinets and printers that are likely to be used for a number of years. In tax speak, such items are called 'plant and machinery' and can be regarded as assets with an enduring value. Where you can use assets over a number of years, HMRC will not allow you to claim the entire cost as an expense. Instead, you must claim allowances called Capital Allowances.

However, as an employee or director, you cannot claim capital allowances for a car, van, lorry, motorcycle or bicycle that you provide. Instead, you have to claim Mileage Allowance Relief – see Section 13 in Chapter 2 for more information.

Also, there are different rules for certain exotic types of plant and machinery such as water efficient equipment, equipment for refuelling cars with natural gas, short life assets and long life assets. An article on these assets will be available on the website in due course.

There are many different Capital Allowances, but the total amount of the allowance claimed over the years you use the asset are usually equivalent to the payment you made to buy the asset, less any money you get if you sell it. You can usually claim all your expenditure on assets in a tax year using the Capital Allowance called the Annual Investment Allowance, but sometimes it may either be better to claim a lesser value over more than one year using a different Capital Allowance, or to save allowances for use in later years. I will explain this in more detail in the 'Fine Tuning' section later in this chapter.

It is not an easy process, so to simplify and help automate the complexities of it, visit our website (http://taxrefundbook1.accountingwisdom.com) to access various resources including tools and spread sheets. There may be a nominal cost associated with each tool, though from time to time, these will be available free of charge. The site will have regular updates so you may want to sign up at http://taxrefundbook1.accountingwisdom.com to be notified by email of any changes.

Following on from the Index in the previous chapter the next section looks in greater detail at this particular area.

18.   Capital Allowances on plant and machinery used

Plant and machinery are in essence those items that would have a working or useable life of two years or more. So generally, these items will cost more per item than your costs or expenses, for example, computer equipment.

The idea is that if the item lasts for two years or more, you should be allowed to deduct the cost bit by bit over the useful life of the item of plant and machinery. This means that for each item, you have to work out first how much to claim this year, and how much to claim in future years. The method of calculation is not straight-forward, so I have developed some tools to help you which you can find on the website at http://taxrefundbook1.accountingwisdom.com.

Tax Tip 15 – It is important to note that these items of plant and machinery must be used when doing some of the primary activities of your job.

 Tax Tip 16 – The allowance cannot be claimed if your employer was willing to pay for the items.

Tax Gem 3 - You can use plant and machinery for personal reasons, unlike other costs of employment. However, if you do so, you will need to apportion the Capital Allowance claimed between business use and personal use, and only claim the business use portion of the total, maximum possible Capital Allowance. You only need to estimate the proportion that is business use and the difference is personal use.

Tax Gem 4 - When added to other expenses of employment, the total value of expenses together with Capital Allowances are allowed to exceed your

employment income i.e. you can use Capital Allowances to create a loss –
see Section **"Losses Caused by Capital Allowances – a reminder"** in Chapter
Five, "Tricks and tips"

Is record keeping important?

Good record keeping is not just important: it is essential. Keep copies of all
invoices (where available) and record what you used and purchased, what
you use or used it for, whether it was 100% business usage or a proportion
of it. Always record where, when, and how much you purchased the item
for. The date and cost can be especially important to work out which
allowance you can claim. You can write these details on the face of the
invoice to keep it simple.

You can download record keeping spread sheets at
http://taxrefundbook1.accountingwisdom.com.

What types of Capital Allowances can I currently claim?

See flow chart below for a visual aid

The rules for this type of claim change regularly: usually when the
Chancellor announces his Annual Budget, and as of recently also his Autumn
Statement. However it is safe to say you can usually claim one of the four
following types of Capital Allowances:

Annual Investment Allowances (AIA)

You can claim 100% of the cost in the year you bought the item subject to a limit. Here, the calculation is easy as you can claim the entire cost in one year. Be careful, though, as there are limits as to how much you can claim. From 1 January 2013 the limit is £250,000 per year but prior to that, and since its inception in 2008/09, it has ranged from £25,000 to £100,000. See the table below entitled '**Table of Capital Allowance rates and limits**', and the website for more information. Sign up to our update service to be notified when rates and allowances change at http://taxrefundbook1.accountingwisdom.com

If you do spend more than the limit, then you can claim Writing Down Allowances on the amount over the limit so all things being equal, if you spend £300,000, you can claim AIA of £250,000, and claim WDAs on £50,000 to reduce the income on which you pay tax.

First Year Allowances (FYA)

Up to 2007/08, you can claim First Year Allowances of 40% or 50% (see table 'Table of capital allowance rates and limits' below) on money spent on Plant and Machinery considered an asset. After claiming a First Year Allowance, there would be a value of that asset on which you have not claimed a Capital Allowance, i.e. 50% in 2007/08. You can claim the rest of the cost by using Writing Down Allowances in future years. For further clarification, visit the website at http://taxrefundbook1.accountingwisdom.com.

Writing down allowances (WDA)

You can claim around 20% of the residual value of the asset each year. The actual rate is currently 18%, but has been up to 25% in prior years. (See table below)

So what is a residual value? The residual value of an asset in your tax return will be the cost of the asset less any Capital Allowances (if any) you have already claimed for that/those asset/s in previous years.

Here is an example. If you bought a computer worth £2,000 in 2011/12, and you didn't claim any FYAs or AIA, then in 2011/12 you would claim a WDA of £400 (£2,000 cost x 20% WDA rate in 2011/12). The residual value of the asset at the end of 2011/12 will be the cost less any allowances claimed i.e. £1,600 (£2,000 - £400). You can carry forward this residual value to use in 2012/13. In 2012/13, you could claim a WDA of £288 being 18% WDA on the residual value brought forward of £1,600. At the end of 2012/13, the residual value of the computer will be £1,312 (£1,600 - £288), and so the process continues. Visit the website for spread sheets and tools to help you with this calculation http://taxrefundbook1.accountingwisdom.com.

NB You can claim the WDA for any assets that you have not claimed an AIA.

What if I have many assets?

If you have many assets, you can group them together in one lump called a 'Pool' so you don't have to do a separate calculation for each asset. Each year you can add new assets you have not claimed AIA on into this Pool. You can then claim 18% Writing Down Allowances on the residual value of the total Pool.

Alternatively, you can keep each asset separate and formulate a separate calculation for each asset. (See Balancing Allowances below)

Small Pool Write Off (SPWO)

If the amount left on your Pool after claiming WDAs is £1,000 or less, then you can claim the entire balance as well, to bring the Pool value down to £0.

Low value items

Where these items only have a low value, you can claim all of their cost as an expense, and not a capital allowance e.g. cheap pocket calculators, staplers, hole punches.

This chart here helps clarify the point.

Table of Capital allowance rates and limits

Type	Exception	2012/13	2011/12	2010/11	2009/10	2008/09
Annual investment allowance (AIA)		100%	100%	100%	100%	100%
AIA annual limit	£250,000	£25,000	£100,000	£100,000	£50,000	£50,000
	From 1/1/2013					
First year allowance (FYA)	-	N/A	N/A	N/A	N/A	N/A
Writing down allowance (WDA) - general pool	-	18%	20%	20%	20%	20%
Small pool write off, written down balance in either or both WDA pool(s) is £1,000 or less	-	100%	100%	100%	100%	100%

How to work out your capital allowance claim – the normal situation

- Total up what you spent on plant and machinery during the tax year (up to 5 April), then deduct any contribution from your employer and the amount of any personal use (**Capex**).

- If the amount is less than the AIA, then claim the amount you spent, less any contribution from your employer, less the amount of personal use.

- If the amount you spent, less any contribution from your employer, less the amount of personal use is more than the AIA, then claim the maximum AIA, and claim Writing Down Allowances on the balance, as noted below.

- If you intend to lump all the remaining assets together with the residual Pool value from last year (if there is a Pool), then add the two sums together to arrive at the 'New Pool'. If the sum is less than £1,000, then claim the full £1,000. If the New Pool sum is more than £1,000, then calculate the Writing Down Allowance to claim as around 18% (check the website for up to date rates) and then include this figure in your claim for the year. Finally calculate the residual value of the Pool, which will be the New Pool less your WDA claim for the year.

If you intend to calculate your Writing Down Allowances on each asset separately, go to the website for more information, help and further tools.

[SAR "Employment" pages E1 →Employment expenses →Box 20 "Other expenses and capital allowances" or in any similar box.]

Flow charts to help you claim Capital Allowances

Basic data required

A. How much did you spend on assets?

    a. Deduct any contribution from your employer, and the amount of any personal use of the asset.

    b. The balance is your allowable value (**Capex**).

B. What is your Total Taxable Income? (**TTI** which is the income from all sources after deductions of relevant costs as appropriate and might also include bank interest, dividend income, business profits and so on)

C. What is your personal allowance for the year? (**PA**)

D. What is the Residual Value, in any, of your assets brought forward from last year? (**RV**)

E. What WDA can you claim on the RV of assets brought forward from last year? (**WDARV**)

Warning: These are simplified flowcharts that should be applicable for most employees. However, if your needs are more complex, or you have many assets, you should seek further help.

Flowchart 1: If you purchased assets this year and have no residual values from last year (no FYA)

Is the Capex (A) > Total taxable income (TTI) less personal allowance (PA)?

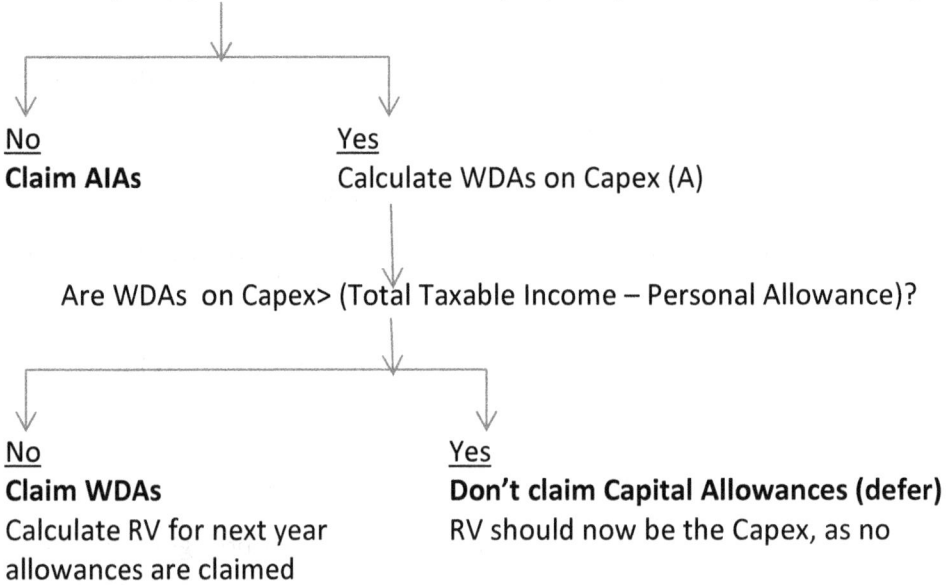

No
Claim AIAs

Yes
Calculate WDAs on Capex (A)

Are WDAs on Capex> (Total Taxable Income – Personal Allowance)?

No
Claim WDAs
Calculate RV for next year allowances are claimed

Yes
Don't claim Capital Allowances (defer)
RV should now be the Capex, as no

Flowchart 2: If you purchased assets this year, and have some residual values from last year (no FYA)

Is the Capex > (TTI – PI)?

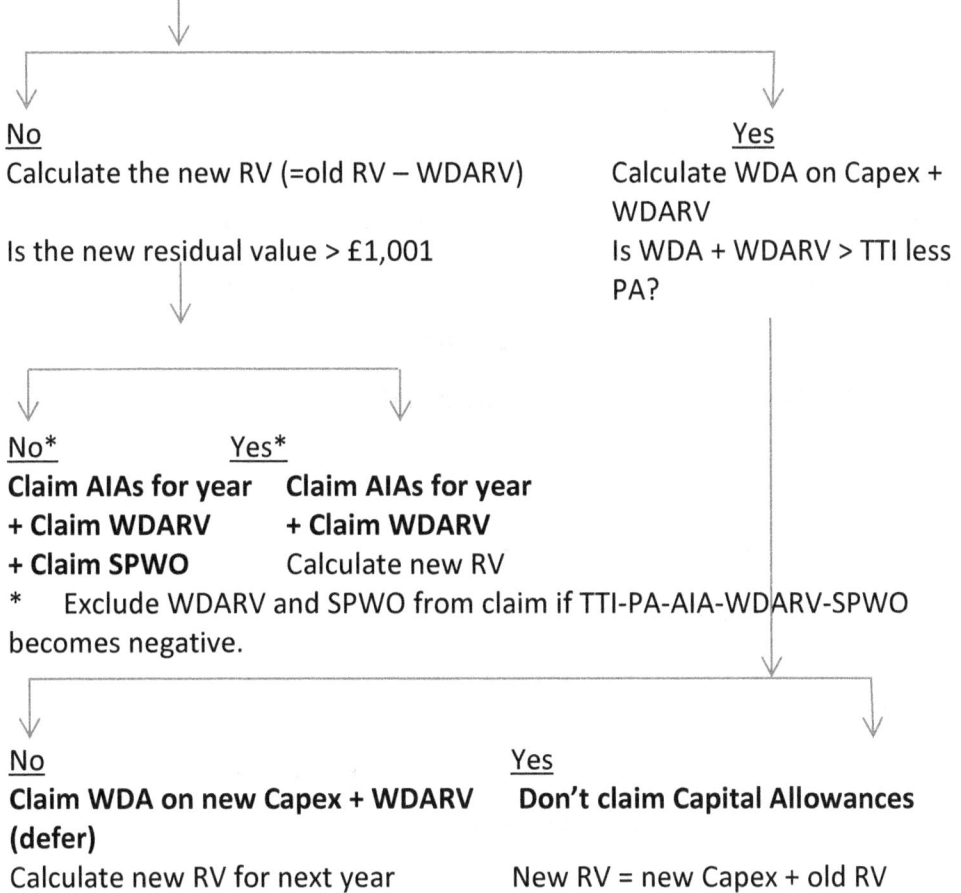

No
Calculate the new RV (=old RV – WDARV)

Is the new residual value > £1,001

    No*   **Yes***
Claim AIAs for year   **Claim AIAs for year**
+ Claim WDARV   **+ Claim WDARV**
+ Claim SPWO   Calculate new RV
*   Exclude WDARV and SPWO from claim if TTI-PA-AIA-WDARV-SPWO becomes negative.

No
Claim WDA on new Capex + WDARV (defer)
Calculate new RV for next year

Yes
Calculate WDA on Capex + WDARV

Is WDA + WDARV > TTI less PA?

Yes
Don't claim Capital Allowances

New RV = new Capex + old RV

Fine-tuning and how to use capital allowances to your benefit

Balancing allowances: What happens when you write off, sell, or dispose of an asset?

If you sell an item of plant and machinery, or cease to use it in your employment if, for example your employment ends, then you will need to work out what are the balance of Capital Allowances that remain on that asset or Pool i.e. the residual value or the asset or pool. You could then potentially either make a claim for a Balancing Allowance or you may have to tell HMRC that you have over claimed and that you owe them a Balancing Charge.

How it works depends on whether you included the item in the Pool or kept a separate calculation each year.

If you kept a separate calculation for that asset, you need to deduct the Disposal Proceeds (see below) from the residual value of the item. If the balance is positive (i.e. RV is greater than the Disposal Proceeds), claim the difference as an allowance (Balancing Allowance). If the value is negative, you will have to tell HMRC that you have over claimed and that a Balancing Charge is due, and tell them the value you have over claimed i.e. the negative value (RV-Disposal Proceeds).

If you included the asset in the Pool, then deduct the Disposal Proceeds (see below) from the residual value of the Pool. If the balance (the reduced residual value) is still positive, use the reduced Pool residual value to calculate Writing Down Allowances for the year. If the value is negative, that shows that you have over-claimed Capital Allowances, and a Balancing Charge (the negative value) needs to be given back to HMRC i.e. you will have to tell HMRC that you have over claimed and that a Balancing Charge is due. You can only get a Balancing Allowance on the Pool if you are selling the last asset left.

The Disposal Proceeds are either

- The net proceeds from the sale of the asset after deducting cost of selling the asset

or

- the estimated value of the asset if you haven't sold it, but have ceased to use it for your employment.

For example: if you sold the your computer for £1,000 in 2013/14, when the residual value was £1,312, then as the residual value is more than the cash you received, you can claim a Balancing Allowance of £312 (£1,312 residual value less £1,000 cash received on sale). If however, you sell it for £1,500, then £1,312 - £1,500 = -£188 i.e. you will owe HMRC a Balancing Charge of £188.

[*You note this in SAR "Employment" pages E1* →*Employment expenses* →**Box 20** **"Other expenses and Capital Allowances" or in any similar box.**]

Creating losses if you have other income sources

By using Capital Allowances, you reduce your taxable income and so reduce the tax you pay. Unlike all other costs that employees and directors are allowed to claim, this can create a situation where your total deductions (allowances & expenses) exceed your employment income, and so can create a loss. The loss is akin to saying that HMRC owe you money, in addition to a refund of any income tax you paid that year. You can request that some or all of the excess ('loss') to be set off against your other income for example dividends, rental income, bank interest and so on, to reduce the tax you should pay on that other income.

Tax Tip 17 – Use this only if you have other sources of income in addition to your employment income. If you do not have any other sources of income you should consider "Not claiming your Capital Allowances" this year. See the next item.

For more information, discussions, and worked examples, go to the website http://taxrefundbook1.accountingwisdom.com.

Not claiming Capital Allowance to protect your Personal Allowance

Consider not making a claim until your Total Income is greater than your Personal Allowance. If your Total Income is less than your Personal Allowance then don't make a claim as you will lose the value of your

Personal Allowance for the year. Rather, keep the residual value of your assets higher so you can make a greater claim for Capital Allowances the following year. **Please note:** Total Income will include your income from your employer, and any other income you receive in the form of taxable bank interest (not ISA), dividends, rental income, trading income, capital gains and so on. For more information, discussions, and worked examples, go to the website http://taxrefundbook1.accountingwisdom.com.

Motorbikes, cars, bicycles, and accessories

If you use your own bicycle, car, motorcycle, or van for business purposes, you will have to claim Mileage Allowance Relief to get credit for the use of your own vehicle – see Section 13 of Chapter 2 entitled 'Travelling: allowance for using your own vehicle – Mileage Allowance Relief (MAR)'. You cannot claim Capital Allowances on any of these modes of transport.

You can, however, claim Capital Allowances on mobile telephones, car telephones and in-car entertainment if you have a travelling appointment, and your contracted duties require that you should be in contact, or be able to be in contact with others on a continual basis for business purposes.

19. Interest on certain loans

You can claim the cost of interest on loans used to purchase plant and machinery if you can claim Capital Allowances on that particular item or items. The interest you claim should be the amount due during the tax year.

Your claim should be reduced if you use the asset for personal reasons by the same percentage or fraction used to calculate your Capital Allowance.

To aid this process, you should ask your loan provider for a statement or written confirmation of the interest you paid between 6 April and the 5 April one year later. If your loan provider will not provide the amount, then you will have to work out the amount based on the price of the asset, and the total payments you will make. Go to the website at http://taxrefundbook1.accountingwisdom.com for calculators to help you work out the interest relating to the year that you can claim.

[*SAR "Employment" pages E1* →*Employment expenses* →**Box 20 "Other expenses and capital allowances" or in any similar box.**]

Other tax effective payments

20.   Gift Aid donations

You can claim the amount you paid in Gift Aid donations during the year and you should keep a record of all Gift Aid donations that you paid. In fact, you should always claim this sum, but this will be of actual benefit if you pay any tax at 40% or more i.e. at the Higher or Additional rates of Income tax.

If you pay money under Gift Aid, a charity will get the benefit of a tax refund at 20% (the basic rate) on the amounts you pay them. If you pay tax at higher or additional rates i.e. 40%, or 45%, then if you make a claim for this, **you will also get a tax refund**.

This is a win win situation courtesy of the UK Government!

Warning! If the amount of tax you pay is less than the value of the gift aid (20%) that the charity receives, you may be required to repay the difference to HMRC!

In Chapter 6, I will show you how to value your donations ready to include on you claim.

In Chapter 5, I show you some extra tricks and tips which could be useful to save even more tax, and one of these relates to Gift Aid donations and is called **Gift Aid Carry Back.**

For more detailed information on how Gift Aid works, together with examples, go to the website page

[*SAR "Tax reliefs" pages TR4* →*Charitable giving* →**Box 5 "Gift Aid payments made in the year to 5 April 2012" or in any similar box.**]

21. Personal Pension Payments

You can make a claim for all pension contributions you make personally to a pension provider. This excludes any payments your employer deducts from your wages for pension before they pay you.

Tax Tip 18 – Please check with your provider whether they claim the tax relief at source, or not

For each pension scheme keep a record of the policy number, the policy provider's name and the total paid each year between 6 April and 5 April in the following year.

This will be of increased benefit if you pay any tax at 40% or more (i.e. at the Higher or Additional rates of Income Tax)

You will then reduce your tax bill or get a refund based on this grossed up value and your top rate of tax. The higher the rate of tax you pay, the more tax relief you will get.

In Chapter 6, I will show you how to value payments made to pension providers ready to include on you claim.

For more detailed information on how this relief for Pensions works, together with examples, go to the website page

http://taxrefundbook1.accountingwisdom.com.

[**_If your pension provider does not claim tax relief at source (normal situation):_**
_SAR "Tax reliefs" pages TR4 →Paying into registered pension schemes and overseas
pension schemes →**Box 2** "Payments to a retirement annuity contract where basic
rate tax relief will not be claimed by your provider_ **" or in any similar box.**]

[**_If your pension provider 'claims tax relief at source':_** _SAR "Tax reliefs" pages
TR4 →Paying into registered pension schemes and overseas pension schemes →
Box 1 "Payments to registered pension schemes where basic rate tax relief will be
claimed by your pension provider (called 'relief at source'). Enter the payments and
basic rate tax"_ **or in any similar box.**]

Chapter Four

Industry and Job-specific Allowances – Costs and Expenses You Can Claim

HMRC makes special allowances for certain industries and jobs. These come in two forms a) Fixed Rate Expenses (FRE) where you use specialist or protective clothing, and/or your own tools, and b) other specific job related allowances.

If you are able to claim these and haven't done so before, you could get a tax refund worth hundreds, or in some cases, thousands of pounds, and you will pay less tax in the future starting from now. That's a lot of benefit!

You can claim these job and industry specific allowances alongside any of the other 19 items set out in Chapter Two & Chapter Three, but you can not claim them twice under different headings.

Do you know whether your job or your industry is entitled to claim special allowances? If not, read through this chapter to see if the list includes your particular profession.

Specialist clothing and tools: what's it all about?

Consider for a moment what clothing you wear when doing your job. If your role requires you to wear a uniform, specialist clothing, protective clothing or clothes and shoes in particular colours, or if you have to buy tools to do your job, you will be able to claim specific allowances every year you are or were employed in that role.

The good news is, you can not only claim 1) the costs you paid to **purchase** the clothing or tools but 2) if you are responsible for **cleaning** them, you can also claim a special and specific allowance called Flat Rate Expenses (FRE) even if you have only spent even £1.

If your employer makes available cash or tokens for cleaning, you should deduct the value of the cash or tokens from the FRE and claim the reduced FRE. You should always deduct this value made available to you by your employer even if you do not use the tokens or claim the cash.

In any year, if you spent more on cleaning than the value of the FRE, you can claim the actual costs you paid. But remember to keep a list of the items, and copies of the receipts, and you will have to write to HMRC each year you want to claim your actual costs.

To help your claim, you should explain to HMRC how you qualify to make this claim, for example why you have to use the clothing or tools you have purchased to do your job, or why your cleaning and maintenance costs are for example greater than normal. For more information, and worked examples of real life cases, read the articles on the dedicated website at http://taxrefundbook1.accountingwisdom.com.

Tax Tip 19 – You can claim these FRE allowances for specialist clothing or tools in addition to the remaining nineteen expenses and allowances noted in Chapter Two and Chapter Three.

Tax Tip 20 – Remember it is possible to claim the actual costs if these are greater than the FREs, but it is necessary to also keep a detailed record of actual expenses if this is the case.

For tools, resources, and Apps to help you keep a record of your expenses go to http://taxrefundbook1.accountingwisdom.com.

Guaranteed tax refunds and less tax in future with just one claim

The FRE is a guaranteed allowance and for every year you do that job you are entitled to a tax refund. This is good news! Not only that but

- You can make the claim today going back up to 5-6 years which could generate a sizeable tax refund.
- Once successfully claimed, HMRC should apply these FREs to all future years, as they are an annual allowance. This means that if you remain in that industry you should pay less tax every year from now on.

Tax Tip 21 – When your claim has been approved, check the Notice of Coding (HMRC form P2) that HMRC send to you to ensure they have included these FREs in future years.

Tax Tip 22 – Remember to tell HMRC if you change your job, or industry and if you are claiming costs and allowances other than FREs, you will need to make a new claim each year when you spend money on those items.

How to go forwards

To help you quickly find your allowance entitlements, I have summarised information from HMRC's website and its Employee Income Manual, and set it out by Industry, then by profession of role within the industry.

So now scan through the following pages looking through each of the two lists to find the job in the industry that most closely matches your role.

If you can't find your industry in the list, look for a similar role using the Index and then see if you can claim the FRE related to that role, or if all else fails, you can claim the "Standard amount" FRE of £60 for the laundry costs of uniforms or protective clothing. You will have to explain to HMRC what you do and why you are entitled to tax relief. If you are successful using this method I would like to use your story in a published case study with your permission. Please email me at taxrefundbook01@accountingwisdom.com and you will be paid £50 for taking part.

If you have to complete a Self Assessment tax Return as part of your claim, [*enter the FRE values in **Box 18 'Fixed deductions for expenses', in the Employment expenses on the SAR 'Employment' pages E1 or in any similar box.*]* For more about SARs, and how to complete them, go to the website http://taxrefundbook1.accountingwisdom.com.

List of job specific allowances, costs, & expenses available, by industry

Agricultural Workers

- All workers can claim an FRE of £100 per annum.

Airline Pilots

- Can claim two thirds of their annual subscriptions to the British Airline Pilots' Association (BALPA).
- Can claim the actual cost of uniforms required to be worn by their employer.
- Can claim the actual cost of noise-cancelling headsets.
- Can claim an FRE of £850 to cover expenses, or the actual cost of the following expenses: uniform cleaning, equipment including torch, CRP5, knee board, Trifold, chart plotters, mileage scale rule, atlas, protractors and dividers, pens, travel iron, calculator, stopwatch, clipboard, sunglasses, reference materials, flight case, currency commission and where necessary, a duplicate passport.
- Can claim a further expense allowance of £100, or the actual cost of travel, to cover travel expenses to the following events: medical examinations, flight simulator sessions, technical refresher sessions, Crew Resource Management training (CRM), Emergency and Safety Equipment training (SEP), Fire and Smoke training (F&S).

Tax Tip 23 – Uniformed flight deck crew, including pilots and co-pilots of helicopters, can also claim specific 'Pilots allowable expenses'.

Tax Tip 24 – Where any actual cost incurred by the individual is greater than £850 (less any untaxed contribution from your employer) it is possible to claim the actual costs.

For Apps and resources to help you keep a track of your expenditure, go to the website http://taxrefundbook1.accountingwisdom.com.

All industries not listed in Index

You can claim the "Standard amount" FRE of £60 for the laundry costs of uniforms or protective clothing.

Aluminium Industry Workers

- Can claim a FRE of £140 if employed as a continual casting operator, process operator, de-dimpler, drier, drill puncher, dross unloader, firemen, furnace operator, furnace operator helper, leader, mould-man, pourer, remelt department labourer, or a roll flattener - "firemen" means persons engaged to light and maintain furnaces.
- Can claim a FRE of £80 if employed as a cable hand, case maker, labourer, mate, truck driver, measurer, or storekeeper.
- Can claim a FRE of £60 employed as an apprentice.
- All other workers can claim an FRE of £120.

Armed Forces

- You can claim the cost of cleaning if you live off base and clean the uniform yourself.

- You can claim the cost of buying uniforms where you have to purchase them yourself.

Armed Forces: Reserve and Auxiliary Forces Members

- Can claim the actual cost of uniform if paid for personally.
- Can claim the cost of cleaning the uniform if paid for personally, and if the employer has not provided an allowance or cleaning vouchers.
- Can claim the cost of travel if home is more than a mile from the duty centre
- Can claim an allowance for travel if their own car, motorcycle, or bicycle is used and home is more than a mile from the duty centre – see Section 13 in Chapter Two on claiming Mileage Allowance Relief (MAR)

Bank and Building Societies Employees

- Can claim the cost they have to pay to purchase the following items of uniform: jackets, trousers and caps, if applicable.
- Can claim the cleaning cost for those same items of uniform jackets if paid for personally.

- **OR** you can claim for an FRE of £60 can be made by uniformed doormen or messengers.

Brass & Copper Industry Employees

- Can claim a FRE of £120 if employed as a brazier, coppersmith, finisher, fitter, moulder, turner and all other workers.

British Telecom Employees

- HMRC have kept this private. Contact them directly for further information, and refer to our website regularly for further updates.

Building and Civil Engineering Employees

- Can receive travel and lodging allowances tax free from their employer under the working rule agreement (see HMRC Notice EIM71300 onwards) of the Construction Industry Joint Council (CIJC).

Tax Tip 25 – If you have to pay more than the value of the tax-free Travel & Lodging Allowance, claim the difference. See also the Section 15 in Chapter Two on Travel Expenses.

Building Industry Workers

- Can claim a FRE of £140 if employed as a joiner or carpenter.

- Can claim a FRE of £80 if employed as a cement worker, roofing felter or asphalt labourer.
- Can claim a FRE of £60 if employed as a labourer or navvy.
- All other workers can claim an FRE of £120.

Building Materials Industry Workers

- Can claim an annual FRE allowance of £120 if employed as a stonemason.
- Can claim an annual FRE allowance of £60 if employed as a tile-maker or labourer.
- All other workers can claim an annual FRE allowance of £80.

Car Mechanics

- You can claim the cost of the tools (where tools are required to undertake tasks, and for which the employer has not provided, but which have been purchased personally), either 1) over a number of years as a capital allowance, or 2) in the year of acquisition as either an Annual Investment Allowance, or 3) as a S336 ITEPA 2003 deduction i.e. as an expense of employment.

- For more information about claiming the costs of tools in the year of acquisition see Chapter Three (Capital Allowances) and Chapter Five (Tricks and tips - **Losses Caused by Capital & Allowances Deferring Capital Allowances**).

Clergy and Ministers of Religion

As an employee, or an office holder, of a particular church or congregation, it is possible to claim the following expenses and allowances if appropriate.

- Up to 25% of 'the rent paid for a dwelling house, any part of which is used mainly and substantially for the purposes of' all duties.
- Up to 25% of the expenditure on the maintenance, repair, insurance or management of any accommodation that is made available to the employee if they perform the duties of their employment from the accommodation.
- Other costs specific to the role and calling.

Tax Tip 26 - If you are neither employed by a particular church or congregation, nor hold office with a particular church or congregation, then your income will be classed as trading. Please refer to the webpage http://taxrefundbook1.accountingwisdom.com for more information.

Clothing Industry Workers

- Can claim a FRE of £60 if employed as a lace maker, hosiery bleacher, dyer, scourer, knitter, knitwear bleacher or dyer.
- All other workers can claim an annual FRE of £60.

Constructional Engineering Industry Workers

- Can claim a FRE of £140 if employed as a blacksmith, striker, burner, caulker, chipper, driller, erector, fitter, holder up, marker off, plater, rigger, riveter, rivet heater, scaffolder, sheeter, template worker, turner or welder.
- Can claim a FRE of £80 if employed as a banks-man, labourer, shop-helper, slewer or straightener.
- Can claim a FRE of £60 if employed as an apprentice and storekeeper.
- All other workers can claim an FRE of £100.

Constructional engineering means engineering undertaken on a construction site, including buildings, shipyards, bridges, roads and other similar operations.

Docks and Inland Waterways - Public Service

See **Public Service - Docks and Inland Waterways** below.

Doctors (medical)

- Can claim the cost of purchase, and the cost of repair and maintenance of loose tools and apparatus used if they are classed as hospital, medical and dental staff, and provide professional services outside the scope of their contract of employment. Costs of purchase should be claimed as Capital Allowances (See Chapter

Three, and Chapter Five), and costs of maintenance, repair, and cleaning should be claimed as expenses of employment (See Section 17 in Chapter Two)

- Can claim the cost of the business calls if there is a necessary cost of telephone calls made in the performance of specific duties.
- Can claim the line rental element only where there is a genuine business need for a second telephone line at home and that line is used exclusively for business calls.
- Can also claim other items if appropriate – see Section on National Health Service Employees below.

Electrical and Electricity Supply Industry Workers

- Can claim an FRE of £60 if you only have laundry costs related to your uniform or specialist clothing.
- All other workers can claim an FRE of £120.

Trades ancillary to engineering

- Can claim an FRE of £140 if employed as a pattern maker.
- Can claim an FRE of £80 if employed as a labourer, supervisor, or unskilled worker.
- Can claim an FRE of £60 if employed as an apprentice, or storekeeper.

- Can claim an FRE of £120 if employed as a motor mechanic in garage repair shop.

- All other workers can claim an FRE of £120.

Other Engineering Industry Workers

See **Other Engineering Industry Workers** listed alphabetically below.

Entertainers

- Can claim fees paid to agents as deductions out of employment income up to 17.5% of the specific employment income.

Tax Tip 27 - This includes theatrical performers, actors, singers, musicians, dancers, theatrical artists, or individuals employed to perform in any setting for example soap opera stars who choose to do pantomime at Christmas.

Examiners

- Can claim use of home for each week if home is the main place of work. Where the room is not being used exclusively for work, the deduction will be limited to the incremental expenses incurred when working from home. This is currently £4 per week, but HMRC may try to limit it to £2 per week (See HMRC Notice EIM32830).

- Can claim the costs of staff if payment is made by results – see Tax Tip below, and Section One from Chapter Two on Assistants Wages.

Tax Tip 28 – In relation to the costs of staff, if you are seen as an employer for PAYE purposes, you will be required to register with HMRC for PAYE, operate a payroll, deduct PAYE, and submit onerous and copious quantities of information to HMRC. You will be required to register as an employer and operate a PAYE payroll, if you are paying staff at or above the PAYE threshold, if your employee already has another job, they are receiving a state, company or private pension, you are paying them at or above the National Insurance Lower Earnings Limit, or if you are providing them with employee So, *caveat emptor*! Beware!

Fire Service (uniformed fire fighters, & uniformed fire officers)

- Can claim an FRE for laundry of uniforms of £80 – less any tokens or allowances received if uniform is required to be worn when at work, and cleaning costs have to paid.

Fishermen

- Can claim a FRE, or actual costs if they are higher for the upkeep of tools/special clothing etc.

Tax Tip 29 – These FREs are usually set for each specific local port so for more information contact HMRC for details. If it is possible to get a group of fishermen together locally, get in contact via the website, or email info@accountingwisdom.com to see how I can be of further help.

Food Industry Workers

- All workers can claim an FRE of £60.

Footballers: Association Football

- Can claim mileage/travel costs to away matches.
- Can claim mileage/travel costs to meet the bus for away matches.
- Can claim mileage/travel costs from training facility to the home ground.
- Can claim mileage/travel costs for medical & other appointments.
- Can claim mileage/travel costs for public appearances.
- Can claim mileage/travel costs when on loan.

See Chapter Two point thirteen on claiming Mileage Allowance Relief, and visit the website for recording tools and handy Apps http://taxrefundbook1.accountingwisdom.com.

Tax Tip 30 – In relation to travel expenses, the journey from home to the training ground is unlikely to be allowable.

There are many rules in relation to the various types of income an Association Footballer could earn. For more help, please contact taxrefundbook01@accountingwisdom.com.

Footballers: Rugby Football

See **Footballers: Association Football** above.

Forestry Industry Workers

- All workers can claim an FRE of £100.

Glass Industry Workers

- All workers can claim an FRE of £80.

Health Industry Workers

See **National Health Service Employees (All)** below.

Heating Industry Workers

- Can claim an FRE of £120 if employed as a coverer, domestic glazier, heating engineer, lagger, pipe fitter, plumber, or mate for a coverer, lagger, domestic glazier, OR heating engineer.
- All gas workers can claim an FRE of £100.
- All other workers can claim an FRE of £100.

Insurance Agents

- Detailed rules exist in relation to the type of income streams, but in relation to costs, HMRC only note that claims for Capital Allowance on computers and peripherals should be reduced proportionately to take account of the personal use of the asset i.e. you can claim Capital Allowances on the cost of purchasing computers and peripherals. For more information on what can be claimed, and how to make a claim go to Chapter Three and the Capital Allowances and Loan Interest section.

Iron Mining Industry Workers

- Can claim an FRE of £120 if employed as a filler, miner, or underground worker.
- All other workers can claim an FRE of £100.

Iron and Steel Industry Workers

- Can claim an FRE of £80 if employed as a day labourer, general labourer, stockman, timekeeper, warehouse staff, or weighman.
- Can claim an FRE of £60 if employed as an apprentice.
- All other workers can claim an FRE of £140.

Leather Industry Workers

- Can claim an FRE of £80 if employed as a currier (wet worker), fellmongering worker, or tanning operative (wet).
- All other workers can claim an FRE of £60.

Local Government Councillors and Civic Dignitaries

- Can claim travel to and from home, where duties are undertaken at home on behalf of the authority, as it is accepted that councillors normally have two places of work.
- Expenses normally accepted include 1) travelling expenses 2) Mileage Allowance Relief, and 3) other expenses, all incurred wholly exclusively and necessarily in the performance of civic duties.
- Go to Chapter Two for more information on travelling expenses and Mileage Allowance Relief.
- Other expenses can include postage and stationery, telephone costs, secretarial assistance, hire of rooms, household expenses and other sundry expenses.
- For a more detailed walk through key principles to bear in mind when deciding what is possible, go to Chapter One for Key Principles, and Chapter Two for more specific information regarding Travelling Expenses.

Tax Tip 31 – Items can only be claimed for that are not already claimable from the Local Authority.

Lorry drivers

- Can claim the cost of the issue or renewal of an LGV licence (formerly HGV licence)
- Can claim any related medical expense costs (perhaps including travel to and from an examination) in relation to the issue or renewal of an LGV licence.
- Can claim the cost of a digital tachograph card including the cost of photographs used on the card.

Midwives

- Can claim a Use-Of-Home Allowance of £208 (£4 per week in 2013/14), or the actual incremental costs (see Chapter Two section sixteen) if they are domiciliary midwife (i.e. A community midwife attending home confinements in the patients home), and they need to provide a room at their own home to store equipment which cost the employer does not refund.
- Can claim FREs for laundry of £100.
- Can claim FREs for shoes of £12.
- Can claim FREs for stockings, tights, or socks of £8.

Tax Tip 32 – You can claim the Use-of-Home Allowance if your employer has either 1) not paid you any such allowance, or if 2) your employer has paid you an allowance for use of home and it has either been taxed by your employer under PAYE, or if appears on your P11D.

National Health Service Employees (All)

- Can claim a FREs if a uniform and its cleaning costs are required. See the Health Workers table below.

- Can also claim an FRE of £12 per year if specific shoes of a prescribed style are required i.e. if the employer stipulates what colour, or style the shoes should be.

- Can also claim an FRE of £6 per year if specific stockings, tights or socks in a prescribed style or colour are required.

- Below is a Table of FREs available to different categories of NHS, and healthcare staff

Table of FREs available to different categories of NHS, and healthcare staff

Amount of FRE	Applicable NHS and healthcare staff	HMRC Category
£140	Ambulance staff on active service	1
£100	chiropodists, dental nurses, occupational, speech, physiotherapists and other therapists, phlebotomists, radiographers, nurses, midwives	2
£100	Plaster room orderlies, hospital porters, ward clerks, sterile supply workers, hospital domestics, hospital catering staff	3
£60	Laboratory staff, pharmacists and pharmacy assistants, uniformed ancillary staff - maintenance workers, grounds staff, drivers, parking attendants and security guards, receptionists and other uniformed staff	4

North Sea and Other Offshore Oil and Gas Workers

- Can claim "Home to work travel" (mainland departure point) if the rig is a temporary workplace, and there is a substantial effect on the journey.

Nurses

- See section on National Health Service Employees (All) above

Other (Particular) Engineering Industry Workers

Other (Particular) engineering means engineering undertaken on a commercial basis in a factory or workshop for the purposes of producing components such as wire, springs, nails and locks.

- Can claim an FRE of £140 if employed as a pattern maker.
- Can claim an FRE of £120 if employed as a chainmaker; cleaner, galvaniser, tinner and wire drawer in the **wire drawing industry**.
- Can claim an FRE of £120 if employed as a toolmaker in the **lock making industry**.
- Can claim an FRE of £60 if employed as an apprentice or storekeeper.
- All other workers can claim an FRE of £80.

Parish and Community Council Clerks in England and Wales

- Can claim amounts for travel, and other expenses.

Pilots - see **Airline Pilots**

Police Service: Designated Dog Handlers

- Can claim the expenses of travelling with the dog between the handler's home and permanent workplace and, also the nearest suitable place to exercise the dog. The following conditions have to be met: 1) the handler is required to kennel the dog at or near his or her home and is provided with the necessary equipment for doing so; 2) the handler is responsible for grooming, feeding and exercising the dog there and receives a grooming allowance (or equivalent) for doing so; 3) the handler is responsible for the proper control of the dog and its behaviour both on and off duty; 4) the handler lives on premises owned by the Police Authority, or in private accommodation the location of which has been approved by the Police Authority.

Police Service

- Can claim £140 FRE allowance for laundry & cleaning if employed as a Police Officer, or a PCSO.

- Can claim £60 FRE allowance for laundry & cleaning if employed as any other police service employee.

Post Office employees

- Can claim any net cash deficiency (i.e. the balance of deficiencies over excesses) that they, as a sub-postmaster, are required to pay back to the Post Office.

Precious Metals Industry Workers

- All workers can claim an FRE of £100.

Printing Industry Workers

- Can claim an FRE of £140 if employed as a letterpress Section-electrical engineer (rotary presses), electrotyper, ink and roller maker, machine minder (rotary presses), or stereotype.
- Can claim an FRE of £60 if employed as a bench hand (periodical and bookbinding section), compositor (letterpress section), reader (letterpress section), telecommunications and electronic section wire room operator, or warehouseman (paper box making section).
- All other workers can claim an FRE of £100.

Prison Service

- Can claim £80 FRE allowance for laundry & cleaning if employed as a uniformed prison officer.
- Can claim the expenses of travelling with the dog if employed as a designated dog handler. (see Section **Police Service: Designated Dog Handlers** above)

Private Hospitals

- see **National Health Service Employees (All)** above

Public Service - Docks and Inland Waterways Workers

- Can claim an FRE of £80 if employed as a docker, or dredger driver.
- Can claim an FRE of £60 if employed as a hopper steerer.
- All other workers can claim an FRE of £60.

Public Transport Workers

- Can claim an FRE of £80 if employed as a garage hand including cleaner.
- Can claim an FRE of £60 if employed as a conductor, or driver.

Quarrying Industry Workers

- All workers can claim an FRE of £100.

Railway Industry Workers

Look up your role in the Index to see if you can get a higher FRE in a different industry for example engineers, vehicles, etc.

- All other workers can claim an FRE of £100.

Seafarers and Seamen

- Can claim an FRE of £165 if employed as a carpenter on cargo vessels, tankers, coasters and ferries.
- Can claim an FRE of £140 if employed as a carpenter on a passenger liner.

Allowances are available for working gear, renewal or instruments, and upkeep of uniforms as follows (Including Chief Purser, Chief Catering Officer and Chief Radio Officer):

- Can claim an FRE of £135 if employed as a Master, Chief Officer, Chief Engineer, Second Engineer, or Other Officers (including Pursers and Chief Stewards) on a passenger liner.
- Can claim an FRE of £115 if employed as a Master on cargo vessels, tankers or ferries.

- Can claim an FRE of £105 if employed as a Chief Officer, Chief Engineer or Second Engineer on Cargo vessels, tankers or ferries.
- Can claim an FRE of £85 if employed as any Other Officer (including Pursers and Chief Stewards) on cargo vessels, tankers or ferries.
- Can claim an FRE of £75 if employed as a Master, Chief Officer, Chief Engineer or Second Engineer on coasters (except ferries).
- Can claim an FRE of £60 if employed as any Other Officer (including Pursers and Chief Stewards) on coasters (except ferries).
- Can claim the cost of provision of own food *in connection with board* while living away from home, the contract requires that he or she should find their own food.

Seafarer Earnings Deduction

Tax Tip 33 – It could be possible for tax to be paid on only part or none of specific earnings using the Seafarers Earnings Deductions if: all work takes place on a ship; some duties are performed outside of the UK; if at least 6 months of the year is spent away from the UK.

The value of this allowance can run into thousands of pounds so it will be no surprise to know that more detailed and complex rules apply.

Shipyards Industry

- Can claim an FRE of £140 if employed as a blacksmith, blacksmith's striker, boilermaker, burner, carpenter, caulker, driller, furnaceman (platers) holder up, fitter, plater, plumber, riveter, sheet iron worker, shipwright, tuber, or welder.

- Can claim an FRE of £80 if employed as a labourer.
- Can claim an FRE of £60 if employed as an apprentice, or storekeeper.
- All other workers can claim an FRE of £100.

Teachers, Lecturers and Tutors

Claims can be made on the deduction for the cost and/or upkeep of items paid for which are necessary to the performance of duties (connected to your role as a teacher, lecturer, or tutor), if the employer does not already supply the items or pay for such items. This can include:

1. **Specialist clothing** including academic dress and protective clothing, for example, overalls, boots, goggles, helmets, laboratory coats, clothing for use in catering departments, gymnastic dress, PE kit & trainers.
2. **Books** for use in class made available for pupils to use, or used to prepare lectures.
3. **Equipment** including tape recorders, record players, slide rules, calculators, drawing instruments, computers and so on. See Tools and Equipment in Chapter Two, and Capital Allowances in Chapter Three.
4. **Research expenditure** for degree level work.
5. **Secretarial services** in higher education. See Assistants Wages in Chapter Two.

6. **Subscriptions to professional bodies and learned societies** that include technical periodicals already supplied e.g. General Teaching Council for England, NUT, Faculty of Teachers in Commerce, etc

7. **Use of accommodation at home** if in higher education and it can be proven that a study is required by the nature of the role (see contract section) and is not used merely as a matter of convenience. Reasons could include the varied nature of his/her duties, the absence of fixed hours of work, the need to consult extensive and expensive journals and reference books required for the preparation of lectures as well as for research (and which cannot reasonably be kept in a university or college room) and the overcrowding of staff accommodation at universities and colleges. See Section 16 '**Use of home and working from home**' in Chapter Two

8. **Travelling expenses** - see the section on Travel for the basic information. The qualification hurdles are likely to be met if the employee is on a designated and specific travelling appointment. Claimable expenses could include *inter alia* train fares, use of own vehicle (by claiming Mileage Allowance Relief), light refreshments when out, and possibly also accommodation costs.

9. **Computer & other equipment** in higher education where equipment fulfils tasks previously carried out by more laborious means, or where the research itself intrinsically requires the equipment. Refer back to the Section on Capital Allowances in Chapter Two to work out how much to claim and in which year.

Textile and Textile Printing Industry

- Can claim an FRE of £120 if employed as a carder, carding engineer, overlooker, or technician in spinning mills.
- All other workers can claim an FRE of £80.

Tree fellers

- Can claim two classes of costs related to power saws i.e. capital allowances on the purchase of saws in addition to the costs of maintaining power saws.

Vehicles Industry Workers

- Can claim an FRE of £140 if employed as a builder, railway vehicle repairer, or railway wagon lifter.
- Can claim an FRE of £80 if employed as a railway vehicle painter, letterer, builder's assistant or repairers assistant.
- All other workers can claim an FRE of £60.

Tax Tip 34 – This heading applies to all those who work in the vehicles industry, including railway vehicle workers.

Wood and Furniture Industry Workers

- Can claim an FRE of £140 if employed as a carpenter, cabinetmaker, joiner, wood carver, or woodcutting machinist.

- Can claim an FRE of £120 if employed as an artificial limb maker (other than in wood), organ builder, or a packaging case maker.

- Can claim an FRE of £60 if employed as a 'coopers not providing your own tools', labourer, polisher, or upholsterer.

- All other workers can claim an FRE of £100.

Chapter Five

Tricks and tips

By now it should be clear what you can claim for, the value you can claim for, and whether there is an FRE available. So the process is now over half way there.

To go further towards completion, this short chapter is here to help ensure your claim is successful before showing you in the next chapter how to compile and submit your claim.

Check your P11D

In the months of June or July, your employer may give you a form P11D. This form tells HMRC about specific things, other than your salary and pay, that HMRC will tax you on. The form states the tax value of apparent benefits you 'receive' from your employer, which typically includes the use of a company car, private health plan costs paid by your employer, and certain of the expenses you have claimed from your employer that have been refunded to you.

HMRC will tax you on these values through your tax code (that is HMRC's form P2 Notice of Coding) even if, in the case of expenses refunded to you by your employer, you have paid for the items out of your own money.

You will therefore need to make a counter claim to prevent yourself being overtaxed. You should check the P11D carefully, so that you can make a claim to HMRC for your costs of employment to reduce, or cancel, the value of the 'benefits' noted on your P11D.

What should I check my P11D for?

- The items that your employer has paid for directly.
- The items you paid for initially, whose costs were then were reimbursed to you by your employer. If you are in doubt, ask your employer or payroll/HR team to explain what was included.

If an item falls into this second category, you should make a claim for a 'cost of employment' for the same value on the P11D, or the actual amount you paid if your employer did not reimburse you in full for that item. This could be greater than the value on the P11D. See Chapter Six 'How to Make a Claim.'

If the item relates to fuel reimbursed for car mileage on business, then claim the MAR allowance, as this will probably be higher. See Section 13 in Chapter 2 for more information.

Record keeping

It is essential you document your specific role and all the types of costs you incur connected with that role. Write down what you do and how you do it, and if you can, note where this is indicated in your contract. In addition, clarify the job description and the job competencies from your employment manual.

If your role or job has changed, you may need to ask your employer to update your job description or contract of employment.

Then make a note of what expenses you pay which are related to your job description or your working practice, noting which you have to incur e.g. the job description for an accountant may ask for an ACCA qualified accountant, in which case your annual ACCA professional subscription can be claimed. Likewise if you are employed as a forklift truck driver then the cost of obtaining and renewing your forklift truck licence will be allowed.

Keep a careful record of all expenses you have paid for anything to do with your employment, noting the date, supplier, purpose of the expense, and the value. This includes a record of all mileage used on specified dates to specified destinations. You can keep a record on paper or use spread sheets and even a mobile phone App. Go to page http://taxrefundbook1.accountingwisdom.com for up to date information on the latest apps available to help you.

If you have more than one employer, you are required to set out your costs and match them to each specific job. For more information on the expenses that various professions typically claim, go to the website page http://taxrefundbook1.accountingwisdom.com.

Gift Aid Carry Back

HMRC will allow you to 'carry back' Gift Aid donations to the previous tax year and they will treat the donation as if you made it a year earlier.

Use this if you moved into the higher tax, or additional tax bracket last year by nearly the amount of the Gift Aid donation. This will allow you to pay tax at a lower rate, rather than the higher rates, and so get a tax refund related to the difference between the two if you have already paid the tax.

As this is a retrospective claim, it can help you clean up minor irregularities after the event, but you will have needed to have made the Gift Aid donation before you make the claim. It is important to contact HMRC to tell them that you would like to choose to do this.

Note that you can only use a donation once. If you do elect to carry back your Gift Aid donations to last year, you will not be able to use the donation again in this year.

Don't make this claim if it causes you to pay more tax this year than you will save from last year.

For a worked example, go to our website at

http://taxrefundbook1.accountingwisdom.com

*[**If paid this year, and to be carried back to last year's SAR;** SAR "Tax reliefs" pages TR4 →Charitable giving →Box 7 "Gift Aid payments made in the year to 5 April 2013 but treated as if made in the year to 5 April 2012" or in any similar box.]*

*[**If paid following year, and to be carried back to this year's SAR;** SAR "Tax reliefs" pages TR4 →Charitable giving →Box 8 "Gift Aid payments made after 5 April 2013 but to be treated as if made in the year to 5 April 2013" or in any similar box.]*

Losses Caused by Capital Allowances – a reminder

Unlike costs and expenses that you claim, claiming Capital Allowances, on top of the other types of costs, expenses, and allowances, can cause your income to be negative.

Use this route if you have income or profits from other sources for example bank interest or trading income. You can reduce the other income and total tax you have to pay on all your different sources of income, by using the value of the loss caused by Capital Allowances.

For more detailed information visit the website at http://taxrefundbook1.accountingwisdom.com.

Deferring Capital Allowances – a reminder

Unlike costs and expenses you claim, you can choose not to claim Capital

Allowances in one year, but save them for future years.

Use this route if claiming your Capital Allowances will result in your income being below the level of your personal allowance for the year. It will prevent you losing your tax-free personal allowance for that year.

For more detailed information visit the website at http://taxrefundbook1.accountingwisdom.com.

Chapter Six

How to make a claim

This chapter shows you how to write your claim letter step-by step by providing detailed examples and templates to make sure you don't forget anything, and points out how to make a claim using one of the other three ways set out by HMRC. It will also point you to additional tools and resources to give you more tips and tricks to ensure you have done everything you can to merit a successful claim.

By now you will have listed all the items for which you can claim, worked out the value for each item, made notes on why you can claim each item, cross checked your claim to your P11D if you have one, and you should have double-checked everything.

So now you are ready to make your claim.

If you have to complete a Self Assessment tax Return (SAR)

There are four ways of making a claim for your costs.

The easiest way to make a claim is on a Self Assessment Tax (SAR) Return. However, filling in Self Assessment Tax Returns can be complicated and onerous, and-not all employees are required by HMRC to complete an annual SAR, but if you are required to do so, you will have to complete an annual SAR for each year you had to make a claim! Ouch.

If you are required by HMRC to complete an SAR then read on, otherwise, skip to the next section entitled '**Everyone else & the ideal method**'.

At the end of each section, or type of expense, I have set out a pathway in green to explain which page to go to in your SAR tax return; which section, and in which box to enter the values you have worked out.

E.g. [*SAR "Employment" pages E1 →Employment expenses →Box 20 "Other expenses and capital allowances" or in any similar box*]
In the case above, first go to the 'Employment section' of your SAR tax return e.g. "SA102 2013"; if you submit a paper tax return, this will be page E1. Then, find the section entitled 'Employment expenses'. Finally enter data into Box 20 'Other expenses and Capital Allowances'.

NB Use 'any similar box' with a similar description on the SAR if the box number does not match — HMRC has different versions of the Employment pages for different categories of claimants.

Everyone else & the ideal method

You can submit a claim in a) writing (the ideal), b) using Form P87 (click here http://taxrefundbook1.accountingwisdom.com or go to HMRC's website to find this form) or c) by telephoning the HMRC helpline (for more help go to http://taxrefundbook1.accountingwisdom.com, if you are not required by HMRC to submit a Self Assessment Tax Return.

However, telephoning HMRC can be tricky as they will often use jargon or ask you loaded questions, which could knock you off balance. In addition, you will need to have all the relevant information at hand and there are restrictions on when you can use this service. However, it may be the route you prefer in which case, their contact number is currently 0845 300 0627.

Alternatively, you can download and complete HMRC's form P87 if you want to claim expenses over £1,000, it's the first time you've claimed, or if you're claiming expenses for a year before the previous tax year.

You can download a form P87 from HMRC and for help on how to complete this form, or for more worked examples, articles, and "how to videos" go to the website at http://taxrefundbook1.accountingwisdom.com.

Either way, <u>we recommend</u> that you write the letter, and use it to collect all the information you need ready to call HMRC, or ready to fill in Form P87.

Submitting a claim in writing

I would always advise to make a claim in writing because it is the simplest way to stay in control of the process, and it applies in every eventuality.

Below is information about how to claim, specific templates you will need, and examples of what a completed claim in writing should look like.

On the website you will see there is a **Quickclaim** automated service which, for a small additional fee, prepares your claim letter ready for you to download, print, sign and post at http://taxrefundbook1.accountingwisdom.com. Alternatively, you can use the templates at the back of the book, or download free Word templates from the website at http://taxrefundbook1.accountingwisdom.com.

If you write to HMRC you should currently (as of June 2013) send your letter to HMRC, PAYE & Self Assessments, PO Box 1970, Liverpool, L75 1WX. Your letter should include:

- Your name
- Your National Insurance number
- Your address
- It should state: 'I am making a claim for the following expenses and payments, which may fall under Schedule 1AB TMA 1970 (overpayment relief).'
- For expenses and allowances (excluding Gift Aid, or payments for Pension) if you wish to claim for just the current year, you should note
  - o Your employer's name
  - o Your employer's PAYE reference
  - o Your employer's address
  - o An itemised list of each cost, expense, FRE, or allowance you want to claim

- For expenses and allowances (excluding Gift Aid, or payments for Pension) if you wish to claim for more than just the current year, you should *note for each year*
  - Your employer's name
  - Your employer's PAYE reference
  - Your employers address
  - An itemised list of each cost, expense, FRE, or allowance you want to claim
- For Gift Aid, and for Payments for Pensions, see separate paragraph below for relevant wording & examples.
- State 'The particulars given in this claim are correct and complete to the best of my knowledge and belief.'
- You should also state how you want any tax refunds paid to you. You have two choices a) by cheque, or b) by direct credit. If you want a direct credit, you should also details of the account you want refunds sent to i.e. bank name, bank sort code [*XX-XX-XX*], account number [*XXXXXXX*], name on account [*usually your name*], reference [*if any, or if building society account*].

Templates and examples are available at the back of this book and you can you can download and print them from the website http://taxrefundbook1.accountingwisdom.com.

If you only want to claim FREs, you can use the **QuickClaim** service on the website at http://taxrefundbook1.accountingwisdom.com to prepare and print a completed letter all ready for you to sign and post.

Gift Aid Claims

If you made payments under Gift Aid, and if you pay tax at 40% or above, you should:

1. Total up all the payments you made between 6 April and the following 5 April
2. Calculate the "Grossed Up Value" of the total. This is an easy calculation; simply multiply by 100, then divide by 80.

> For example: £10 per month = £120. £120 of payments made multiply by 100 → £120 X 100 = £12,000 divided by 80 → £12,000/80 = £150.

Note in the claim the following table. You can also add this table to a claim for expenses, and/or pensions depending on what you actually made payments for and are claiming for.

For example, if you paid £10.00 per month only between 6 April 2009 and 5 April 2010, you would include the following table.

Tax year	Purpose of payment	Amount Paid (Net)	Amount paid (Gross) i.e. Grossed up Valued
2009/10	Gift Aid donations	£120.00	£150.00

For more information, resources, and tools visit the website at http://taxrefundbook1.accountingwisdom.com.

Claims for Payment for Pensions

If you made Payments for Pensions to one or more Pension Providers, you should:

1. Note in the claim the name of your pension provider.
2. Note in the claim the policy number.
3. Total up all the payments you made between 6 April and the following 5 April.
4. Calculate the Grossed Up Value of the total. This is an easy calculation; simply multiply by 100 then divide by 80.

> For example: £80 of payments made multiply by 100 → £80 X 100 = £8,000 divided by 80 → £8,000/80 = £100

Note in the claim the following table. You can also add this table to a claim for expenses and/or Gift Aid depending on what you actually made payments and what you are claiming for.

For example, if you paid £80.00 during the year into one pension scheme, and £160.00 into a second pension scheme, between 6 April 2009 and 5 April 2010 only, you would include the following table.

Tax year	Payment made to	Policy number	Amount Paid (Net)	Amount paid (Gross) i.e. Grossed Up Value
2009/10	AvivA	123-456-78	£80.00	£100.00
2009/10	AvivB	123-456-80	£160.00	£200.00

For more information, resources, and tools visit the website at
http://taxrefundbook1.accountingwisdom.com.

Posting documents to HMRC

Tax Tip 35 – Always send items in the post to HMRC by recorded delivery.

Although the law presumes that an item sent by first class post has been sent, HMRC have been known to lose letters, and then, perhaps unlawfully, put the burden of proof on you. So don't risk the anxiety this causes by keeping a copy of all documents and sending everything by recorded delivery. It should only cost you £1 more than the normal postage charge.

How far back can I make a claim?

You can make a claim up to five years after you have incurred the cost up to the annual 5 April deadline. For example, if you make a claim before 5 April 2013 deadline, you can claim expenses back to 6 April 2008 (from the 2008/09 tax year). If you make a claim before 5 April 2014 deadline, you can claim expenses back to 6 April 2009 (from the 2009/10 tax year).

If in doubt, make a claim anyway. After all, if you don't ask, you don't get!

Template Claim Letters you can copy & use

You can get copies of these templates in Word format at http://taxrefundbook1.accountingwisdom.com.

Template Claim Letter for expenses only
Instructions in italic; Send by recorded delivery

[Date of letter]

HMRC,
PAYE & Self Assessments,
PO Box 1970,
Liverpool,
L75 1WX

Dear Sir/Madam,
[Your name]
NINo: **[Your national insurance number]**
Claim for expenses of employment
I am making a claim for the following expenses and payments, which may fall under Schedule 1AB TMA 1970 (overpayment relief).

[Add a paragraph about the role for which you wish to claim these expenses e.g. job title/role, when you started this type of job, name of current employer if relevant].

Table of items I wish to claim

Tax year to 5 April	Name of employer	Employer's PAYE reference	Type of expense being claimed	Amount £.p
e.g. 2011/12	e.g. Tesco	e.g. 123/AB456	e.g. Flat rate expense	

{Please pay any tax that I have overpaid to me by cheque.} – *delete as appropriate*

{Please pay any tax that I have overpaid to me by direct credit to the following bank account at [*name of bank*], sort code [*XX-XX-XX*], account number [*XXXXXXXX*], name on account [*usually your name*], reference [*if any, or if building society account*] .} – *delete as appropriate*

The particulars given in this claim are correct and complete to the best of my knowledge and belief

Yours faithfully,

_____ *Sign here*
[Your name]

[Your address]
[Optional: Your telephone number. Your email address]
www.accountingwisdom.com

97

Example of completed claim letter for expenses only

31 January 2014

HMRC,
PAYE & Self Assessments,
PO Box 1970,
Liverpool,
L75 1WX.

Dear Sir/Madam,
Miss Jane Smith
NINo: JS123456A
Claim for expenses of employment
I am making a claim for the following expenses and payments, which may fall under
Schedule 1AB TMA 1970 (overpayment relief).

I have been employed as an apprentice carpenter since 1 April 2007. I am currently working
for "Jesus of Nazareth Ltd". I am required to wear protective clothing and supply my own
tools.

Table of items I wish to claim

Tax year to 5 April	Name of employer	Employer's PAYE reference	Type of expense being claimed	Amount
2009/10	A Limited	123/ON056	Flat rate expense	30.00
2010/11	S Limited	987/YY654	Flat rate expense	50.00
2011/12	S Limited	987/YY654	Flat rate expense	60.00
2012/13	S Limited	987/YY654	Flat rate expense	60.00
2013/14	S Limited	987/YY654	Flat rate expense	60.00

Please pay any tax that I have overpaid to me by direct credit to the following bank account
at Bank of Crooks, sort code [12-34-56], account number [12346578], name on account [J
M Smith].

The particulars given in this claim are correct and complete to the best of my knowledge
and belief

Yours faithfully,

JSmith
_____
Miss Jane Smith

Blank Template Claim Letter for expenses only

HMRC,
PAYE & Self Assessments,
PO Box 1970,
Liverpool,
L75 1WX

Dear Sir/Madam,

NINo:
Claim for expenses of employment

I am making a claim for the following expenses and payments, which may fall under Schedule 1AB TMA 1970 (overpayment relief).

Table of items I wish to claim

Tax year to 5 April	Name of employer	Employer's PAYE reference	Type of expense being claimed	Amount

Please pay any tax that I have overpaid to me

The particulars given in this claim are correct and complete to the best of my knowledge and belief

Yours faithfully,

_____

Template Claim Letter for Gift Aid payments only
Instructions in italic. **Send by *recorded* delivery**

[Date of letter]

HMRC,
PAYE & Self Assessments,
PO Box 1970,
Liverpool,
L75 1WX

Dear Sir/Madam,
[Your name]
NINo: *[Your national insurance number]*
Claim for expenses of Gift Aid payments
I am making a claim for the following expenses and payments, which may fall under
Schedule 1AB TMA 1970 (overpayment relief).

Tax year	Purpose of payment	Amount Paid (Net)	Amount paid (Gross) i.e. Grossed Up Value
2009/10	Gift Aid donations e.g. £10/month	e.g.£120.00	e.g. £150.00
2010/11			
2011/12			
2012/13			

{Please pay any tax that I have overpaid to me by cheque.} – *delete as appropriate*

{Please pay any tax that I have overpaid to me by direct credit to the following bank
account at *[name of bank]*, sort code *[XX-XX-XX]*, account number *[XXXXXXXX]*, name on
account *[usually your name]*, reference *[if any, or if building society account]* .} – *delete as
appropriate*

The particulars given in this claim are correct and complete to the best of my knowledge
and belief

Yours faithfully,

_____ *Sign here*
[Your name]

[Your address]
[Optional: Your telephone number. Your email address]
www.accountingwisdom.com

100

Example of completed Claim Letter for Gift Aid payments only

31 January 2014

HMRC,
PAYE & Self Assessments,
PO Box 1970,
Liverpool,
L75 1WX.

Dear Sir/Madam,
Miss Jane Smith
NINo: JS123456A
Claim for expenses of Gift Aid payments
I am making a claim for the following expenses and payments, which may fall under
Schedule 1AB TMA 1970 (overpayment relief).

Tax year	Purpose of payment	Amount Paid (Net)	Amount paid (Gross) i.e. Grossed Up Value
2009/10	Gift Aid donations £10/month	£120.00	£150.00
2010/11	Gift Aid donations £11/month	£132.00	£165.00
2011/12	Gift Aid donations £12/month	£144.00	£180.00
2012/13	Gift Aid donations £13/month	£156.00	£195.00

Please pay any tax that I have overpaid to me by direct credit to the following bank account
at Bank of Crooks, sort code [12-34-56], account number [12346578], name on account [J
M Smith].

The particulars given in this claim are correct and complete to the best of my knowledge
and belief

Yours faithfully,

JSmith
_____
Miss Jane Smith

Flat 1, The Grove, London, EC78 90Y
0207 123 4678
www.accountingwisdom.com

Blank Claim Letter for Gift Aid payments only

HMRC,
PAYE & Self Assessments,
PO Box 1970,
Liverpool,
L75 1WX

Dear Sir/Madam,

NINo:

Claim for expenses of Gift Aid payments

I am making a claim for the following expenses and payments, which may fall under Schedule 1AB TMA 1970 (overpayment relief).

Tax year	Purpose of payment	Amount Paid (Net)	Amount paid (Gross) i.e. Grossed Up Value

Please pay any tax that I have overpaid to me by

The particulars given in this claim are correct and complete to the best of my knowledge and belief

Yours faithfully,

_____

Template Claim Letter for pensions only
Instructions in italic. Send by recorded delivery

[Date of letter]

HMRC,
PAYE & Self Assessments,
PO Box 1970,
Liverpool,
L75 1WX

Dear Sir/Madam,
[Your name]
NINo: ***[Your national insurance number]***
Claim for expenses of payments for pensions
I am making a claim for the following expenses and payments, which may fall under
Schedule 1AB TMA 1970 (overpayment relief).

Tax year	Payment made to	Policy number	Amount Paid (Net)	Amount paid (Gross) i.e. Grossed Up Value
e.g. 2009/10	*e.g. Aviva*	*e.g. 123-456-78*	*e.g. £XX*	*e.g. £YY*

{Please pay any tax that I have overpaid to me by cheque.} – *delete as appropriate*

{Please pay any tax that I have overpaid to me by direct credit to the following bank
account at [*name of bank*], sort code [*XX-XX-XX*], account number [*XXXXXXXX*], name on
account [*usually your name*], reference [*if any, or if building society account*] .} – *delete as*
appropriate

The particulars given in this claim are correct and complete to the best of my knowledge
and belief

Yours faithfully,

_____ *Sign here*
[Your name]

[Your address]
[Optional: Your telephone number. Your email address]
www.accountingwisdom.com

Example of completed Claim Letter for pensions only

31 January 2014

HMRC,
PAYE & Self Assessments,
PO Box 1970,
Liverpool,
L75 1WX.

Dear Sir/Madam,
Miss Jane Smith
NINo: JS123456A
Claim for expenses of payments for pensions
I am making a claim for the following expenses and payments, which may fall under
Schedule 1AB TMA 1970 (overpayment relief).

Tax year	Payment made to	Policy number	Amount Paid (Net)	Amount paid (Gross) i.e. Grossed Up Value
2009/10	Aviva	123-456-78	£80	£100
2009/11	Aviva	123-456-78	£88	£110
2011/12	Aviva	123-456-78	£96	£120
2012/13	Aviva	123-456-78	£120	£150

Please pay any tax that I have overpaid to me by direct credit to the following bank account
at Bank of Crooks, sort code [12-34-56], account number [12346578], name on account [J
M Smith].

The particulars given in this claim are correct and complete to the best of my knowledge
and belief

Yours faithfully,

JSmith
_____
Miss Jane Smith

Blank Claim Letter for pensions only
Instructions in italic

HMRC,
PAYE & Self Assessments,
PO Box 1970,
Liverpool,
L75 1WX

Dear Sir/Madam,

NINo:
Claim for expenses of payments for pensions
I am making a claim for the following expenses and payments, which may fall under Schedule 1AB TMA 1970 (overpayment relief).

Tax year	Payment made to	Policy number	Amount Paid (Net)	Amount paid (Gross) i.e. Grossed Up Value

Please pay any tax that I have overpaid to me by

The particulars given in this claim are correct and complete to the best of my knowledge and belief

Yours faithfully,

_____
[Your name]

[Your address]
[Optional: Your telephone number. Your email address]
<u>www.accountingwisdom.com</u>

105

Example of completed Claim Letter for Gift Aid & pensions

31 January 2014

HMRC,
PAYE & Self Assessments,
PO Box 1970,
Liverpool,
L75 1WX.
Dear Sir/Madam,
Miss Jane Smith
NINo: JS123456A
Claim for expenses of payments for Gift Aid & pensions
I am making a claim for the following expenses and payments, which may fall under Schedule 1AB TMA 1970 (overpayment relief).
Table of Gift Aid donations made

Tax year	Purpose of payment	Amount Paid (Net)	Amount paid (Gross) i.e. Grossed Up Value
2009/10	Tear Fund £10/month	£120.00	£150.00
2010/11	Barnados £11/month	£132.00	£165.00
2011/12	Cancer Research £12/month	£144.00	£180.00
2012/13	Local Sports Club £13/month	£156.00	£195.00

Table of pension payments made

Tax year	Payment made to	Policy number	Amount Paid (Net)	Amount paid (Gross) i.e. Grossed Up Value
2009/10	Aviva	123-456-78	£80	£100
2009/11	Aviva	123-456-78	£88	£110
2011/12	Aviva	123-456-78	£96	£120
2012/13	Aviva	123-456-78	£120	£150

Please pay any tax that I have overpaid to me by direct credit to the following bank account at Bank of Crooks, sort code [12-34-56], account number [12346578], name on account [J M Smith].

The particulars given in this claim are correct and complete to the best of my knowledge and belief

Yours faithfully,

JSmith

_____

Miss Jane Smith

Lists of Tax Tips, Tax Gems, Tables, and Templates

List of Tax Tips

List of Tax Tips continued

List of Tax Gems

List of diagrams, flow charts, and tables

Index

Look up your profession, or question, for more ideas that could help you save tax. Page numbers noted after each item.

A

Aluminium industry 57

Car allowances (MAR) 26, 27, 28, 47, 58, 84

Car mechanics 25, 64

Car washing 19

Carder in Textiles & Textile Printing Industry 80

Carding engineer in Textiles & Textile Printing Industry 80

Carpenter (also p97)

In Building Industry 59

In Shipyards Industry 78

In Wood and Furniture Industry 81

On Cargo vessels, tankers, coasters and ferries 76

On Passenger liners 76

Case maker

In Aluminium Industry 57

Wood and Furniture Industry Workers 81

Catering staff in NHS, private, or nursing homes 25, 71, 78

Catering Officer 25, 76, 78

Caulker

Constructional Engineering Industry 62

Shipyards 78

Cement worker in Building Industry 60

Chainmaker in Wire Drawing Industry 72

Chief Engineer 77

On Cargo vessels, tankers and ferries 77

Coding (P2 Notice of Coding) 54, 83, 106

Community support officer in Police Force (PCSO) 74

Compositor (letterpress section) in Printing Industry 74

Conductor in Public Transport 76

Constructional Engineering Industry 62

    All other workers 62

    Apprentice 62

    Banksman 62

    Blacksmith 62

    Blacksmith striker 62

    Burner 62

    Caulker   62

    Chipper   62

    Driller 62

    Erector 62

    Fitter 62

    Holder up 62

    Labourer 62

    Marker off 62

    Plater 62

    Rigger 62

    Rivet heater 62

    Riveter 62

    Scaffolder 62

E

F

M

MAR (Mileage Allowance Relief) 26, 27, 28, 47, 58, 84

Marker off in Constructional Engineering Industry 62

Master Seafrer 76, 77

Mate in Aluminium Industry 57

Mate for a coverer, lagger, domestic glazier, OR heating engineer in Heating Industry 67

Meals & refreshments (look up "subsistence" as well) 28, 29

Measurer in Aluminium Industry 57

Messenger in Banks and Building Societies 59

Midwives in NHS, private, or nursing homes 32, 70, 71

Midwives 32, 70, 71

Midwives - domicilliary / community in NHS, private, or nursing homes 32, 70, 71

Mileage Allowance Relief (MAR) 26, 27, 28, 47, 58, 84

Miner in Iron Mining Industry 68

Ministers of Religion 24, 61

Motor mechanic in garage repair shop - Trades ancillary to engineering 64

Motorcycle allowance 26, 27, 33, 47, 58

Moulder in Brass and Copper Industry 59

Mould-man in Aluminium Industry 57

N

O

Other police employees in Police Force 74

Other therapists in NHS, private, or nursing homes 71

Other uniformed staff in NHS, private, or nursing homes 71

Overlooker in Textiles & Textile Printing Industry 80

P

P11D 13, 22, 27, 28, 71, 82, 83, 88

Form P87 90

Packaging case maker in Wood and Furniture Industry 81

Parish and Community Council Clerks in England and Wales 73

Parking attendants – uniformed in NHS, private, or nursing homes 71

Pattern maker

    Other (Particular) Engineering 72

    Trades ancillary to engineering 63

Pension payments 17, 50, 51, 65, 91, 92, 93, 94, 102, 103, 104, 105, 106

Personal Allowance 41, 42, 46, 47, 87

Pharmacist IN NHS, private, or nursing homes 71

Pharmacy assistant in NHS, private, or nursing homes 71

Phlebotomist in NHS, private, or nursing homes 71

Physiotherapist in NHS, private, or nursing homes 71

Pilots - see Airline pilots 26, 56, 57, 73

Pilots (uniformed) in Airline Industry 26, 56, 57, 73

Pipe fitter in Heating Industry 67

Plaster room orderly in NHS, private, or nursing homes 71

Plater

    Constructional Engineering Industry 62

    Shipyards Industry (2 options) 78

Plumber

    Heating Industry 67

    Shipyards Industry 78

Police Service

    Community support officer 74

    Designated Dog Handlers 73

    Other police employee 74

    Police officer (ranks up to and including Chief Inspector) 74

Police service, designated dog handlers 73

Polisher in Wood and Furniture Industry 81

Post Office employees 23, 74

Pourer in Aluminium Industry 57

Precious Metals Industry All workers 74

Printing Industry 74

    All other workers 74

    Bench hand (periodical and bookbinding section) 74

    Compositor (letterpress section) 74

    Electrotyper 74

    Ink and Roller maker 74

Railway vehicle painter in Vehicles Industry 80

Railway vehicle repairer in Vehicles Industry 80

Railway wagon lifters in Vehicles Industry 80

Railways 76

All other workers 76

See the appropriate category for professions & craftsmen (for example engineers, vehicles, etc.)

Reader (letterpress section) in Printing Industry 74

Receptionists – uniformed in NHS, private, or nursing homes 71

Record keeping 12, 26, 27, 36, 84

Remelt department labourer in Aluminium Industry 57

Repairer's assistant in Vehicles Industry 80

Residual value (RV) of assets 38, 40, 41, 42, 43, 44, 45, 47

Rigger in Constructional Engineering Industry 62

Rivet heater in Constructional Engineering Industry 62

Riveter

Constructional Engineering Industry 62

Shipyards 78

Roll flattener in Aluminium Industry 57

Roofing felter in Building Industry 60

S

Form SA100 7, 8

Standard amount for the laundry costs of uniforms or protective clothing for all industries not listed here 20, 55, 57

Stereotyper in Printing Industry 74

Sterile supply worker in NHS, private, or nursing homes 71

Stockman in Iron and Steel Industry 68

Stone mason in Building Materials Industry 60

Storekeeper

Aluminium Industry 57

Constructional Engineer in Industry 62

Other (Particular) Engineering Industry 73

Shipyards 78

Trades ancillary to engineering 63

Straightener in Constructional Engineering Industry 62

Subsistence 11, 16, 21, 23, 28, 29

Supervisor in Trades ancillary to engineering 63

T

Tanning operative (wet) in Leather Industry 69

Tax gem 7, 27, 30, 35, 106, 107

Tax refund 2, 6, 7, 49, 52, 54, 85, 92

Tax tip 7, 65, 106, 107

Teachers, lecturers, and tutors 18, 78, 79

Technicians in spinning mills in Textiles & Textile Printing Industry 80

Telecommunications and electronic section wire room operator   in Printing Industry 75

Telephone costs 16, 24, 29, 47, 63, 69

Template worker in Constructional Engineering Industry 62

Textiles & Textile Printing Industry 80

   All other workers 80

   Carder 80

   Carding engineer 80

   Overlooker 80

   Technicians in spinning mills 80

Tilemaker in Building Materials Industry 60

Timekeeper in Iron and Steel Industry 68

Tinner in Wire Drawing Industry 72

Tools & equipment 16, 25, 52, 53, 54, 60, 62, 65, 66, 97

Toolmaker in Lock Making Industry 72

Total Taxable Income (TTI) 41, 42, 43

Trades ancillary to engineering Industry 63, 64

   All other workers 64

   Apprentices 63

   Labourer 63

   Motor mechanic in garage repair shop 64

   Pattern maker 63

   Storekeeper 63

U

V

Van allowance 26, 27, 28, 47, 58, 84

Vehicles Industry 80

 All other workers 80

 Builders 80

 Builder's assistant 80

 Letterer 80

 Railway vehicle painter 80

 Railway vehicle repairer 80

 Railway wagon lifters 80

 Repairer's assistant 80

W

Ward clerk in NHS, private, or nursing homes 71

Warehouse staff in Iron and Steel Industry 68

Warehouseman (paper box making section) in Printing Industry 75

WDA (Writing Down Allowances) 37, 38, 39, 40, 41, 42, 43, 45

Weighman in Iron and Steel Industry 68

Welder

 Constructional Engineering Industry 62

 Shipyards 78

Wire drawer in Wire Drawing Industry 54

Wire drawing industry 72, 73

 Chainmaker 72

 Cleaner 72